TEACHING STUDENTS
WITH
GIFTS AND TALENTS

A Practical Approach to Special Education for Every Teacher

The Fundamentals of Special Education
A Practical Guide for Every Teacher

The Legal Foundations of Special Education
A Practical Guide for Every Teacher

Effective Assessment for Students With Special Needs
A Practical Guide for Every Teacher

Effective Instruction for Students With Special Needs
A Practical Guide for Every Teacher

Working With Families and Community Agencies to Support Students With Special Needs
A Practical Guide for Every Teacher

Public Policy, School Reform, and Special Education
A Practical Guide for Every Teacher

Teaching Students With Sensory Disabilities
A Practical Guide for Every Teacher

Teaching Students With Medical, Physical, and Multiple Disabilities
A Practical Guide for Every Teacher

Teaching Students With Learning Disabilities
A Practical Guide for Every Teacher

Teaching Students With Communication Disorders
A Practical Guide for Every Teacher

Teaching Students With Emotional Disturbance
A Practical Guide for Every Teacher

Teaching Students With Mental Retardation
A Practical Guide for Every Teacher

Teaching Students With Gifts and Talents
A Practical Guide for Every Teacher

TEACHING STUDENTS
WITH
GIFTS AND TALENTS

A Practical Guide for Every Teacher

BOB ALGOZZINE
JIM YSSELDYKE

CORWIN PRESS
A SAGE Publications Company
Thousand Oaks, California

For information:

Corwin Press
A Sage Publications Company
2455 Teller Road
Thousand Oaks, California 91320
www.corwinpress.com

Sage Publications Ltd.
1 Oliver's Yard
55 City Road
London EC1Y 1SP
United Kingdom

Sage Publications India Pvt. Ltd.
B-42, Panchsheel Enclave
Post Box 4109
New Delhi 110 017 India

Printed in the United States of America

Library of Congress Cataloging-in-Publication Data

Algozzine, Robert.
Teaching students with gifts and talents: A practical guide for every teacher / Bob Algozzine and James E. Ysseldyke.
   p. cm.
Includes bibliographical references and index.
ISBN 1-4129-3953-4 (cloth)
ISBN 1-4129-3906-2 (pbk.)
   1. Gifted children—Education—United States. 2. Talented students—Education—United States. I. Ysseldyke, James E. II. Title.
LC3993.9.A75 2006
371.95'6—dc22   2006001783

This book is printed on acid-free paper.

06 07 08 09 10 9 8 7 6 5 4 3 2 1

Acquisitions Editor:	Kylee M. Liegl
Editorial Assistant:	Nadia Kashper
Production Editor:	Denise Santoyo
Copy Editor:	Colleen Brennan
Typesetter:	C&M Digitals (P) Ltd.
Indexer:	Kathy Paparchontis
Cover Designer:	Michael Dubowe

Contents

About *A Practical Approach to Special Education for Every Teacher*   vii
Acknowledgments   viii

About the Authors   xi

Self-Assessment 1   1

Introduction to *Teaching Students With Gifts and Talents* 5

1. **Which Students Do We Consider Gifted and/or Talented?**   9
   Federal Legislation   9
   Varying State Definitions   11
   Identification of Students With Gifts and Talents   12

2. **What Characteristics Are Associated With Gifts and Talents?**   15
   Cognitive   15
   Academic   18
   Physical   20
   Behavioral   21
   Communication   21

3. **What Should Every Teacher Know About Teaching Students With Gifts and Talents?**   23
   Enrichment   23
   Acceleration   25
   Enrichment Tactics   28
   Acceleration Tactics   36

4. **What Trends and Issues Influence How We Teach Students With Gifts and Talents?**   41
   The Evolving Concept of Giftedness   41
   Moving Beyond Intelligence Tests   42
   Underrepresented Groups in the Gifted and
      Talented Category   44
   Tips for Teachers   45

5. **Gifts and Talents in Perspective**   47

6. **What Have We Learned?**   51
   Key Points   51
   Key Vocabulary   52

Self-Assessment 2   55

Answer Key for Self-Assessments   59

On Your Own   61

Resources   63
   Books   63
   Journals   64
   Organizations   65

References   67

Index   69

About
A Practical Approach to Special Education for Every Teacher

S pecial education means specially designed instruction for students with unique learning needs. Students receive special education for many reasons. Students with disabilities such as mental retardation, hearing impairments (including deafness), speech or language impairments, visual impairments (including blindness), emotional disturbance, orthopedic impairments, autism, traumatic brain injury, other health impairments, or specific learning disabilities are entitled to special education services. Students who are gifted and talented also receive special education. Special education services are delivered in many settings, including regular classes, resource rooms, and separate classes. The 13 books of this collection will help you teach students with disabilities and those with gifts and talents. Each book focuses on a specific area of special education and can be used individually or in conjunction with all or some of the other books. Six of the books provide the background and content knowledge you need in order to work effectively with all students with unique learning needs:

Book 1: The Fundamentals of Special Education

Book 2: The Legal Foundations of Special Education

Book 3: Effective Assessment for Students With Special Needs

Book 4: Effective Instruction for Students With Special Needs

Book 5: Working With Families and Community Agencies to Support Students With Special Needs

Book 6: Public Policy, School Reform, and Special Education

Seven of the books focus on teaching specific groups of students who receive special education:

Book 7:   Teaching Students With Sensory Disabilities

Book 8:   Teaching Students With Medical, Physical, and Multiple Disabilities

Book 9:   Teaching Students With Learning Disabilities

Book 10: Teaching Students With Communication Disorders

Book 11: Teaching Students With Emotional Disturbance

Book 12: Teaching Students With Mental Retardation

Book 13: Teaching Students With Gifts and Talents

All of the books in *A Practical Approach to Special Education for Every Teacher* will help you to make a difference in the lives of all students, especially those with unique learning needs.

ACKNOWLEDGMENTS

The approach we take in *A Practical Approach to Special Education for Every Teacher* is an effort to change how professionals learn about special education. The 13 separate books are a result of prodding from our students and from professionals in the field to provide a set of materials that "cut to the chase" in teaching them about students with disabilities and about building the capacity of systems to meet those students' needs. Teachers told us that in their classes they always confront students with special learning needs and students their school district has assigned a label to (e.g., students with learning disabilities). Our students and the professionals we worked with wanted a very practical set of texts that gave them the necessary **information about the students** (e.g., federal definitions, student characteristics) and specific **information on *what to do about* the students** (assessment and teaching strategies, approaches that work). They also wanted the opportunity to purchase parts of textbooks, rather than entire texts, to learn what they needed.

The production of this collection would not have been possible without the support and assistance of many colleagues. Professionals associated with Corwin Press—Faye Zucker, Kylee Liegl, Robb Clouse—helped us work through the idea of introducing special education differently, and their support in helping us do it is deeply appreciated.

Faye Ysseldyke and Kate Algozzine, our children, and our grandchildren also deserve recognition. They have made the problems associated with the project very easy to diminish, deal with, or dismiss. Every day in every way, they enrich our lives and make us better. We are grateful for them.

About the Authors

Bob Algozzine, PhD, is Professor in the Department of Educational Leadership at the University of North Carolina at Charlotte and project codirector of the U.S. Department of Education–supported Behavior and Reading Improvement Center. With 25 years of research experience and extensive firsthand knowledge of teaching students classified as seriously emotionally disturbed (and other equally useless terms), Algozzine is a uniquely qualified staff developer, conference speaker, and teacher of behavior management and effective teaching courses.

As an active partner and collaborator with professionals in the Charlotte-Mecklenburg schools in North Carolina and as an editor of several journals focused on special education, Algozzine keeps his finger on the pulse of current special education practice. He has written more than 250 manuscripts on special education topics, authoring many popular books and textbooks on how to manage emotional and social behavior problems. Through *A Practical Approach to Special Education for Every Teacher,* Algozzine hopes to continue to help improve the lives of students with special needs—and the professionals who teach them.

Jim Ysseldyke, PhD, is Birkmaier Professor in the Department of Educational Psychology, director of the School Psychology Program, and director of the Center for Reading Research at the University of Minnesota. Widely requested as a staff developer and conference speaker, he brings more than 30 years of research and teaching experience to educational professionals around the globe.

As the former director of the federally funded National Center on Educational Outcomes, Ysseldyke conducted research and provided technical support that helped to boost the academic performance of students with disabilities and improve school assessment techniques nationally. Today he continues to work to improve the education of students with disabilities.

The author of more than 300 publications on special education and school psychology, Ysseldyke is best known for his textbooks on assessment, effective instruction, issues in special education, and other cutting-edge areas of education and school psychology. With *A Practical Approach to Special Education for Every Teacher,* he seeks to equip educators with practical knowledge and methods that will help them to better engage students in exploring—and meeting—all their potentials.

Self-Assessment 1

Before you begin this book, check your knowledge of the content being covered. Choose the best answer for each of the following questions.

1. A term used to refer to people with superior intellectual or cognitive abilities is:

   a. Exceptional

   b. Gifted

   c. Talented

   d. Advanced

2. The term that describes people who show outstanding performance in a specific area such as the performing or visual arts is:

   a. Phenomenal

   b. Gifted

   c. Talented

   d. Outstanding

3. Legislation that provides states financial incentive to develop programs for students who are gifted and talented is:

   a. P. L. 99–457

   b. P. L. 94–142

   c. P. L. 95–561

   d. P. L. 95–142

4. What percentage of the total school-age population is estimated to be gifted and/or talented?

   a. 1–3 percent

   b. 3–5 percent

   c. 5–10 percent

   d. 10–15 percent

5. Regarding state legislation for educational programs for students who are gifted and talented:

   a. Educational services are provided in very few states.

   b. Educational services are left up to the discretion of local school districts.

   c. Educational services are mandated in all states.

   d. Educational services are mandated in some states.

6. Common cognitive traits associated with giftedness are:

   a. Rapid generalization, slow comprehension of abstract concepts

   b. Rapid generalization, poor memory

   c. Diminished comprehension of simple relationships

   d. Rapid generalization, quick comprehension of abstract concepts

7. Students who perform well on measures of _____ thinking are usually thought of as creative individuals.

   a. Convergent

   b. Abstract

   c. Complex

   d. Divergent

8. Students who perform well on measures of _____ thinking are thought to show academic aptitude.

   a. Convergent

   b. Abstract

   c. Complex

   d. Divergent

9. Thinking that involves reasoning ability, memory, and classification is:

   a. Convergent

   b. Abstract

   c. Complex

   d. Divergent

10. Individuals who have the skill of flexible thinking are able to:

   a. Produce many words, a variety of associations, phrases, and sentences

   b. Offer a variety of ideas and alternate solutions to problems

   c. Use rare responses and unique words

   d. See alternative solutions ahead of time

REFLECTION

After you answer the multiple-choice questions, think about how you would answer the following questions:

- What factors might affect the academic success of individuals with gifts and talents?

- What differentiates individuals with gifts and talents from other exceptional people?
- What do effective teachers do to provide support for students with gifts and talents?

Introduction to Teaching Students With Gifts and Talents

Lenny is one of those students whose abilities baffle his teachers. At 10 years of age, he scored a perfect score of 800 on the math portion of the Scholastic Aptitude Test. He set a record with four perfect performances on the American High School Math Exam, and he won a gold medal at the International Math Olympics. But Lenny's abilities go beyond mathematics. He has taken honors in violin and piano competitions, played on a championship basketball team, and earned a 4.0 grade-point average in college courses he took while still a full-time high school student. When Lenny enters Harvard at the age of 16 as a sophomore, there is little doubt that his academic career will be an outstanding success.

◦✐◦

Sarah is the best chess player in her class, in her school, and in her hometown. When she finishes the tournaments planned during her third-grade school year, she may be the best chess player in the country. Sarah is good at everything that takes place in school. Her teacher struggles to keep a step ahead of her, especially in math, but she enjoys the challenges that Sarah provides. She knows the school principal plans to offer accelerated coursework to Sarah in a few years, and she hopes Sarah's new teachers will think highly of the work she has done with Sarah.

(Continued)

(Continued)

Nicholas had always been an excellent creative writer. Most of his teachers described him as the "most gifted writer" they have ever taught. By the age of 12, he was writing pieces that most teachers thought were characteristic of much older students. For the first quarter of his eighth-grade year, Nicholas was an excellent student. His teachers were surprised when his parents decided to enroll Nicholas in a special school. They were not surprised because the school was for gifted students but because they thought Nicholas was happy at his present school. When they asked Nicholas's parents why he was moving, they said he was bored with school and didn't enjoy what he did there. They said Nicholas tolerated the work he was assigned because he didn't want his teachers to feel bad. They also described Nicholas's real passion, a biography of Eleanor Roosevelt that he was working on every day after school. Nicholas's teachers described an instructional approach in which students "buy back" school time they were supposed to "spend" in one way so they can spend it in another, and asked his parents to give them a chance to try it before making the school transfer. After a month's participation in this "curriculum compacting" project, Nicholas decided to stay in his neighborhood school.

Gifted, creative, and talented are terms teachers use to describe students like Lenny, Sarah, and Nicholas. Some people use *genius* to refer to them because their strengths are far beyond even those of their peers who are perceived as smart, bright, or artistic. These are students who can solve problems in traditional and nontraditional ways and who demonstrate consistently high performance in areas requiring considerable mental ability. They also come up with novel solutions that are characterized as "creative," "imaginative," "outstanding," and "brilliant" by very talented judges in their respective fields.

These students are recognized and considered exceptional because of the contributions they make and the performances they demonstrate. Widely acknowledged figures from the past and present whose contributions are considered far beyond the ordinary include Maya Angelou, Celestino Beltram, Alexander Calder, Marie Curie, Charles Darwin, Albert Einstein, Duke Ellington, Sigmund Freud, Martha Graham, Harvey Itano, Ynez Mexia, Sir Isaac Newton, Alwin Nikolais, Pablo Picasso, Srinivasa Ramanujan, Chu Shin-Chieh, Igor Stravinsky, Andy Warhol, and Laura Ingalls Wilder. Many believe today's students who are gifted and talented will also make outstanding contributions as they progress through life.

1

Which Students Do We Consider Gifted and/or Talented?

Although a large number of the students in any school are thought to be very smart, only a few are formally identified as gifted and talented. The terms are used to designate people who are intellectually, creatively, academically, or otherwise superior to a comparison group of peers or older students. The term **gifted** is usually used to refer to people with superior intellectual or cognitive performance, whereas the term **talented** is usually used to refer to people who show outstanding performance in a specific area such as the performing arts or visual arts. The terminology typically used in the professional literature to describe students who are gifted and talented is presented in *Table 1.1.* Notice that the terms are generally more positive than those sometimes associated with categories of disability. Notice also that some terms—the positive as well as the negative—may reinforce tendencies to stereotype students who are gifted and talented.

FEDERAL LEGISLATION

"Gifted and talented" is not included in Public Law 94–142 (Education for All Handicapped Children Act) or the Individuals

Table 1.1   Terms Used in the Literature to Describe Students
Who Are Gifted or Talented

abstract thinker	less willing to cooperate or
advanced comprehender	compromise
bookish	motivated
cooperative	natural leader
creative	persistent
daydreamer	precocious
disruptive	prefers to think in
divergent thinker	generalities
erratic	problem solver
evaluative	responsible
flexible	self-critical
good memorizer	sensitive
happy-go-lucky	spontaneous
highly verbal	understands quickly
high tolerance for ambiguity	unmotivated
immature	willing to take mental
intelligent	and emotional risks
intuitive	

With Disabilities Education Act. Separate legislation, the Gifted and Talented Children's Education Act of 1978 (Public Law 95–561), gives states financial incentives to develop programs for students considered gifted and talented. The legislation includes the following definition:

> The term "gifted and talented" means children, and whenever applicable, youth who are identified at the preschool, elementary, or secondary level as possessing demonstrated or potential abilities, that give evidence of high performance capability in areas such as intellectual, creative, specific academic, or leadership ability, or in the performing and visual arts and who by reason thereof require services or activities not ordinarily provided by the school. (Section 902)

The 1978 Gifted and Talented Children's Act was repealed, but many states continue to use its federal definition of gifted and talented. Note the focus on multiple dimensions (intellectual, specific aptitudes, leadership, and arts), inclusion of students who are potentially gifted, and the call for differentiated educational services.

In the past 25 years, many state and federal policies have supported widespread public interest in setting up special programs to serve students who are gifted and talented. Nevertheless, many of the programs that were prevalent in the 1970s and 1980s have been cut back as a result of budget problems (Larsen, Griffin, & Larsen, 1994). Today, a modest federal program, established by the Jakob K. Javits Gifted and Talented Students Act of 1988 (Public Law 100–297), supports demonstration projects, a national research center, and national leadership activities, with priority funding going to efforts to serve gifted and talented students who are economically disadvantaged, speak limited English, or have disabilities.

VARYING STATE DEFINITIONS

State Department of Education personnel write definitions and criteria for identification of students as gifted and talented (Gallagher & Coleman, 1992). In some states, the definition and criteria include both gifted and talented; in others, the two conditions are differentiated. For example, the Annotated Code of Maryland § 8-201–8-204 outlines provisions for gifted and talented education. Maryland defines gifted and talented students as:

> an elementary or secondary student who is identified by a professionally qualified individual as having outstanding abilities in the area of: general intellectual capabilities; specific academic aptitudes; or the creative, visual, or performing arts. (Maryland Department of Education, 2001)

In Louisiana the conditions of gifted and talented are given separate definitions in accordance with R.S. 17:1941 et seq. and the Board of Elementary and Secondary Education, LR 26: 1599:

Gifted—children or youth who demonstrate abilities that give evidence of high performance in academic and intellectual aptitude.

Talented—is possession of measurable abilities that give evidence of unique talent in visual and/or performing arts. (Louisiana Department of Education, 2000)

IDENTIFICATION OF STUDENTS WITH GIFTS AND TALENTS

Note one other distinction in the definitions. The Maryland definition specifically includes the notion of **educational need**, but the Louisiana definitions do not. The concept of educational need is prominent in other state definitions, criteria, and regulations and is central to definitions of many categories of exceptional students.

The *Minnesota Standards for Services to Gifted and Talented Students* (Minnesota State Advisory Council for the Gifted and Talented, 1988) includes an appendix with a list of characteristics of gifted and talented students and a description of the educational need related to each characteristic. The *Minnesota Standards* also include descriptions of individual students who are gifted and talented, to serve as examples of students who should be identified. Three of these descriptions follow so that you may have a better understanding of the types of students identified in definitions of gifted and talented.

1. Chu

Chu is a high school student. He is a Vietnamese immigrant who came to the United States at age 9. He learned to speak English. His fifth-grade teacher noticed his artistic and musical abilities, and he was encouraged to develop these talents. Chu loved designing intricate paper patterns and enjoyed learning. His teacher noticed a very mature sense of humor. Although new to the English language, his humor was dry and he understood the nuances of language missed by many of his age-peers. He was particularly advanced in mathematics and was fascinated with computers.

Encouraged by a mentoring teacher in junior high, Chu succeeded in learning to program a computer and won three national contests sponsored by a national computer firm. There were outlets for his talent. His coursework included independent study and frequent communication with his teacher/ mentor, who shared his interest in computers. Chu's interest in economics was sparked by a community volunteer who sought him out and provided additional support.

His exceptional ability in computer science was supported by individualized attention at his school. Chu was lucky. The high school in his attendance area has a technology focus. The mentoring teacher happened to share his interest and donated her time to work with him. The community volunteer heard about Chu and wanted to help. He needed support, the tools to learn, and an educational climate that recognized and valued his talent and provided outlets for his work. Chu's talent in computer science was appropriately matched with his school program. At the heart of this program was the mentoring teacher who devised an individualized plan to challenge him.

2. Annette

Annette is a highly creative and artistic fifth grader. Her family is very supportive, although they are somewhat bewildered by her disorganized, erratic approach to school work in contrast to her sister, who is well organized and a "teacher pleaser." Her greatest skills and most intense interests are in art and writing. Annette draws incessantly, often instead of doing assignments. She seldom takes the initiative to write a story, although when she receives a writing assignment, she begins with gusto and proceeds far beyond normal expectations. She does not cooperate with all school tasks. She complains about "old facts" (things she already knows), and she is excited by new information.

Annette's life is marked by passionate involvement with drawing, creative fantasy, and a wide interest in a variety of subjects. Her peers respect her drawing skills and sense of humor. Her passionate discourses command their attention, but she is not a sought-after playmate. She changes the rules of the game to use her creativity, and her peers regard this action as cheating. Annette lacks athletic skill. She has been identified for a gifted and talented program designed to challenge her abilities. Annette's classroom teacher also provides special challenges that involve her artistic and creative ability.

3. Elmer

When he entered kindergarten, **Elmer** was reading at a third-grade level. In mathematics he was able to read numbers in the trillions and he could add and subtract. He took pride in recalling populations and land sizes around the world. His kindergarten teacher provided him with more difficult work in reading and mathematics. Elmer still thought kindergarten was a waste of his time. His kindergarten year was also a year in which he formed his opinion on abortion, divorce, world peace, and war. Elmer became depressed and talked about wishing he were dead. Elmer was withdrawn from school, and his mother taught him for the first and second grades.

At the end of second grade, his family moved to a new school district which would provide an individualized plan and allow for some acceleration. At his new school Elmer was given a battery of achievement tests and scored consistently at the eighth- and ninth-grade levels. Currently a fourth grader, Elmer is enrolled in science and mathematics classes with eighth graders. His language arts instruction is provided with a tutor. He attends the remaining classes with other fourth graders. His mental health began to improve when he began to receive a more correct academic diet.

However, Elmer still notes many days of feeling bad about himself and the world. He is very introspective. He receives less encouragement and fewer pats on the back than other children. People assume that someone with his ability has it "all together." His parents continue to be concerned about his mental health. They have arranged for psychological counseling and have actively sought an intellectual peer for him. Elmer is an "at-risk" student, and his psychological and cognitive growth continues to be a serious concern.

2

What Characteristics Are Associated With Gifts and Talents?

I n the sections that follow, we describe the cognitive, academic, physical, behavioral, and communication characteristics of students who are gifted and talented. When you observe
students consistently exhibiting these characteristics, the likelihood that they are gifted and talented is strong. Students
suspected of being gifted and talented may exhibit many, but not
all, of these characteristics and sometimes they exhibit concomitant problems as a result of them. Representative characteristics
and potential problems of students who are gifted and talented
are presented in *Table 2.1*.

COGNITIVE

Rapid generalization and quick comprehension of abstract
concepts and complex relationships are cognitive traits com-
monly associated with giftedness. All learning, "bookish" or
otherwise, involves generalization. Although children, adults,

Table 2.1   Characteristics and Potential Problems of Students Who Are Gifted and Talented

Area	Characteristics	Potential Problems
Cognitive	Outstanding memory Much information Higher-level, abstract thinking Preference for complex and challenging tasks Simultaneous thinking Unusual information processing abilities Creativity	Boredom with pace of instruction Impatience Perceived as showoff by other students Too many questions Resistance to conventional approaches to instruction
Academic	High performance Ease in learning even complex content High problem-solving ability High content mastery	Alienation from peers Expectations from parents for achievement in all areas Resistance for repetitive tasks Classroom disruption when work is complete
Physical	Discrepancies between physical and mental abilities	Limited development of other abilities
Behavioral	Unusual sensitivity to needs of others Sharp sense of humor Unusual intensity	Especially vulnerable to criticism High need for success Perfectionism

Area	Characteristics	Potential Problems
	Persistent, goal-directed orientation	Intolerance and rejection from peers Perceived as stubborn
Communication	Higher level of language development Excellent listening and speaking vocabularies	Alienation from peers Perceived as showoff

and animals generalize in the process of learning, students who are gifted and talented do so more quickly, on the basis of fewer experiences, and more extensively.

Students who are gifted and talented can quickly understand abstract symbols and can uncover complex relationships among the symbols they learn. They differ from other students in the degree of abstractness of the symbols they learn very quickly and in the complexity of the relationships among symbols they learn. They generally have excellent memories and learn facts about concepts like diffusion, justice, homogeneity, and positivism more rapidly and easily than their peers. They comprehend complex relationships like balance, symbiosis, photosynthesis, and equality more easily than do most of their classmates and many students who are older. Sometimes all of these abilities cause problems such as boredom, resistance to conventional instruction, and peer alienation.

One of the cognitive traits regularly associated with giftedness is creativity. There has been much debate about whether creativity is an intellectual trait. Some children and adolescents who earn high scores on intelligence tests also earn high scores on measures of creativity. Yet creativity is not a characteristic of all gifted students, and not all those who perform well on measures of creativity also perform well on intelligence tests. Educators often distinguish two types of thinking: convergent and divergent. Students who perform well on measures of **divergent thinking** are usually thought of as creative. They demonstrate fluency (produce many words, a variety of associations, phrases, and sentences), flexibility (offer a variety of ideas and alternative solutions to problems), originality (use rare responses and unique words), and foresight (see alternative solutions ahead of time). Those who perform well on measures of **convergent thinking** (measures of reasoning ability, memory, and classification) are thought to show high academic aptitude. The traits can be either independent or overlapping. Most often, they overlap: Those who perform well on measures of creativity also perform well on traditional aptitude measures.

Joseph Renzulli is an educator who has repeatedly challenged school personnel to broaden their thinking about giftedness, adding to the concept of giftedness the notion of task commitment (dedicated practice, desire to carry out important work, perseverance). Renzulli (1979) described giftedness as represented by the intersection of three cognitive traits: above-average ability, creativity, and task commitment. According to Renzulli, a major characteristic of individuals who are gifted is consistent high-level performance on tasks.

ACADEMIC

People who are gifted are often first recognized for superior achievement in one or more school subjects. Their performance in mathematics, language arts, science, social studies, or other academic content areas is generally well above average (which means representative of the top 5–10 percent) when compared to their agemates. Often they demonstrate superior abilities in creative and other areas as well (such as photography), and sometimes they excel in very specific aspects of a field of study (e.g., portrait photography or photographic journalism). Learning even complex content comes easier to these students than it does to their peers.

Not all students who are gifted and talented perform well in school. Often their superior abilities create interpersonal problems with peers (such as not wanting to be different and thus trying to be as "normal" as possible). A major line of national research has addressed the problem of gifted students who drop out of school or perform very poorly in school. It has been argued that students who are gifted often drop out of school because the instruction is not challenging enough. As a result, they are not motivated to perform well in school, are victims of poor teaching, and learn to underachieve. The paradox is that students usually are not formally identified as gifted and provided special education services unless they perform well academically. In most states students have to perform significantly above grade level academically, in addition to earning high scores on intelligence tests, to be considered gifted.

Students who are gifted and talented also do not perform at high levels in all school subjects, which sometimes causes problems when parents and others expect uniformly high achievement. For example, it repeatedly has been shown that students who are gifted perform especially well on measures of paragraph meaning, social studies, and science, but that their performance on measures of mathematics is more often at or slightly above grade level. This finding is understandable. Many children learn to read independently of school experience, and once they learn basic decoding skills, they can read very high–level texts. Most students' progress in mathematics is limited by their exposure to, or formal instruction in, mathematics skills. Gallagher (1985) provides an explanation for this observed difference in performance:

> Once the basic skills of reading have been learned, there are almost no additional barriers that need to be surmounted before the youngsters can go ahead, often on their own, in rapidly improving their breadth of knowledge and skill. Their performance on achievement tests, linked to reading, requires no further learning of skills.
>
> However, in the area of arithmetic, achievement is measured by the student's ability to progress through a series of a well-defined hierarchy of skills. Thus, the third-grade child, in order to attain a score in arithmetic computation at the sixth-grade level, would not necessarily have to have great depth of mathematical knowledge but merely knowledge of such arithmetic operations as subtraction of fractions or long division. (p. 39)

PHYSICAL

There is a generally held stereotype of students who are gifted as gangly and physically uncoordinated. No evidence exists for this contention, but pop culture and contemporary trends (such as the image of a "nerd") sometimes perpetuate it. Terman and Oden (1951) reported the results of their longitudinal study of gifted children and stated that "the average member of our group is a slightly better physical specimen than the average child" (p. 23). But even when gifted students are similar in appearance to other students, the stereotype may affect people's perceptions and expectations. For example, many people who are gifted and talented complain that it is difficult to live a "normal" life when everybody expects them to do *everything* well simply because they do *something* well. Others argue that their average physical and athletic abilities are looked down on when compared to superior abilities in other areas (e.g., cognitive or academic skills).

Gallagher (1985) illustrates the point that gifted students are not always physically different with this example:

> If the approximately three million children of 12 years of age were lined up on the interstate highway from New York, they could form a line extending all the way to Chicago. If a teacher then drove from New York to Chicago, he could get a reasonably good picture of the physical characteristics of the children. Suppose that the youngsters whom we have called academically gifted children tied red bandanas around their necks; we could then get some general impression of whether, on the average, they tended to be larger or heavier than the other children without bandanas. If someone came to the teacher after this interesting drive and asked him or her what he thought about the physical characteristics of gifted children, the teacher might very well say, "Well, I thought they were a little bit heavier than the other children." At the same time, however, the teacher would remember the very thin, scrawny boy east of Toledo who, although he had a red bandana around his neck, didn't fit the general statement that the teacher had just made. (pp. 32–33)

BEHAVIORAL

Most professionals argue that it is not meaningful to describe, or be concerned about, the social abilities or the emotional adjustment of children and young adults who are gifted because they vary so widely. Nevertheless, there are many stereotypes of the behavioral characteristics of students who are gifted and talented. Most prevalent is the notion that these students are "eggheads" who do not get along well socially with their peers and classmates. Often people think of students who are gifted as social isolates, and even as weird. Most research contradicts this stereotype, finding that students who are gifted and talented are socially popular and enjoy relatively high social status, but concomitant problems related to their needs and abilities to succeed do exist.

Students who are gifted and talented have unique social and emotional needs of which teachers should be aware and work toward meeting. The affective demands of these students include the need to be stimulated through association with peers and through interaction with adult models and the need to learn to accept their own abilities. Students who are gifted also need to learn to accept their roles as producers of knowledge and creative works; they need to develop habits of inquiry and research and also independence in investigation. It is not uncommon for students who are gifted, and who are not sufficiently challenged by their teachers and the educational experiences they are given, to remain socially aloof, to do just enough in school to get by, and to avoid the difficulty of meeting high teacher and parent expectations.

COMMUNICATION

Students who are gifted and talented typically communicate at a higher level than their same-age peers. They tend to associate and communicate with other children and adolescents who communicate at their level. Imagine you are listening to student conversations about economic issues in a high school class. Groups can carry on conversations about similar topics at different levels; for example, one group might be talking about the cost of living and about whether they will ever make enough money to live comfortably. Another group might be interested primarily in economic policy and discuss the ways in which the laws of supply and demand affect the cost of living, the availability of goods, and so on.

Because students seek their own levels in communicating, students who are gifted and talented often enjoy conversations with adults or older peers more than other agemates. This has an effect on natural social groupings in and across classrooms and is important to consider when grouping students for instructional purposes. It is also a source of potential problems when students who are gifted and talented are seen as showoffs and alienated by their classmates and peers.

3

What Should Every Teacher Know About Teaching Students With Gifts and Talents?

The history of efforts to develop gifts and talents in students is usually traced to the Greeks, who, in working toward full development of the talent of the ablest among their population, established programs for students who were intellectually superior. In today's educational system, students who are gifted and talented are served through two kinds of instructional approaches:

Enrichment

Acceleration or advancement

General tips for working with students who are gifted and talented using these intervention approaches are presented in *Table 3.1.*

ENRICHMENT

The term **enrichment** is used when teachers provide experiences or activities that are beyond the standard curriculum. Early

Table 3.1   Top Ten Tips for Teachers of Students Who Are
Gifted and Talented

1. Provide alternative instructional activities addressing student interests and preferences; celebrate diversity.

2. Provide guest speakers, field trips, practical demonstrations, and other enrichment activities.

3. Model higher-level thinking skills and creative problem-solving approaches.

4. Develop instructional activities that generate problems requiring different types of thinking and solutions.

5. Allow students to move through the curriculum at their own pace.

6. Identify advanced content and assign independent reading, projects, worksheets, reports, and other enrichment activities.

7. Provide opportunities and an environment for sharing novel ideas and solutions to practical problems.

8. Allow students who are gifted to have input in deciding how classroom time is allocated.

9. Provide and encourage independent learning opportunities.

10. Eliminate material from the curriculum that students have mastered.

efforts to educate students who were gifted and talented consisted entirely of enrichment efforts. One of the earliest formal enrichment programs was established in the Cleveland, Ohio, public schools in 1922. Students in enrichment programs are given more work or they are given assignments that extend their knowledge beyond what their peers are learning. They usually stay in their assigned classrooms and typically are enrolled in the same grades as their agemates. Enrichment can involve more than within-class tinkering with the curriculum. Students who are gifted can attend special programs at other schools, or they can be allowed to participate in university programs that help extend their learning.

ACCELERATION

Gifted students also have been treated by **acceleration** or **advancement**, sometimes characterized by double promotion, skipping grades, or advanced enrollment in higher-level coursework. This instructional approach is generally one of changing placement (and thus curriculum or level) rather than modification within a placement. In 1867, the St. Louis, Missouri, public schools began a practice of "flexible promotion." This very early effort to provide advancement for students who were gifted and talented allowed them to be promoted early. More recent evidence of advancement is provided in school districts like the Minneapolis, Minnesota, public schools, where elementary, middle, and high school students who are gifted and talented are allowed to take courses at the University of Minnesota. In other districts, they participate in afterschool classes at the university as evidence of acceleration and advancement.

Point of View:
National Association for Gifted Students (NAGC)

Position Paper: Acceleration

Educational acceleration is one of the cornerstones of exemplary gifted education practices, with more research supporting this intervention than any other in the literature on gifted individuals. The practice of educational acceleration has long been used to match high-level student general ability and specific talent with optimal learning opportunities. The purposes of acceleration as a practice with the gifted are (1) to adjust the pace of instruction to the students' capability in order to develop a sound work ethic, (2) to provide an appropriate level of challenge in order to avoid the boredom from repetitious learning, and (3) to reduce the time period necessary for students to complete traditional schooling. Acceleration benefits many highly capable individuals by better motivating them

(Continued)

(Continued)

toward schooling, enhancing their involvement with extracurricular activities, promoting more challenging options in the middle school and high school years, and preparing them to begin contributing to society at an earlier age. While not as widely used as a practice with diverse gifted learners, evidence suggests that it can be a successful strategy with low income, minority, and students with learning problems as well. Therefore, NAGC strongly endorses this practice as one important avenue to address the needs of gifted learners.

Acceleration practices involve allowing a student to move through traditional educational organizations more rapidly, based on readiness and motivation. Research documents the potential academic benefits and positive outcomes of all forms of appropriately implemented acceleration strategies for intellectually gifted and academically talented learners. These research-based best practices include grade skipping, telescoping, early entrance into kindergarten or college, credit by examination, and acceleration in content areas through such programs as Advanced Placement (AP) and International Baccalaureate (IB) at the high school level. Instructional adaptations in the classroom such as compacting, which allows for more economic use of learning time in a specific subject, are also a desirable and best practice for talented students.

Both group and individual decisions can be made in respect to accelerative options. For example, both AP and IB programs by virtue of their structure and content offer college-level work. As long as students meet prerequisites and accept the rigors of such programs, gifted and other learners can and should take advantage of such group-oriented programs. At an individual level, students may be tutored or engage in online coursework at an accelerated level. Such options can be more readily tailored for individual needs.

Talent search programs at selected universities provide early assessment of advanced mathematical and verbal abilities in students such that decisions on appropriate accelerative options can be constructed inside and outside of schools. For example, several acceleration opportunities can be accessed through online coursework in specific content areas or offered at university sites. Advanced Placement as an accelerative option may be made available throughout the high school years or earlier through independent study, tutorials, or special classes.

Acceleration options should be available at each stage of development in a child's educational program from early entrance to primary school up through early college entry in order to even out the curriculum challenge. Parents may also wish to seek out accelerative opportunities beyond the school setting in order to accommodate an individual student need that cannot be met in traditional school settings.

Yet acceleration decisions should be made thoughtfully with the needs of the whole child in mind. In decision-making about the appropriateness of a particular form of acceleration and the extent of acceleration for a given child at a given time, educators and parents should consider the child's intellectual and academic profile, socio-emotional and physical development, and preferences and dispositions of the child relative to the decision since acceleration may not always be the appropriate option for every gifted child. Factors that enhance the success of acceleration practices include (1) positive attitudes of teachers, (2) timelines related to the decision, (3) parental support, and (4) careful monitoring of the implementation.

Highly able students with capability and motivation to succeed in placements beyond traditional age/grade parameters should be provided the opportunity to enroll in appropriate classes and educational settings. The National Association for Gifted Children program standards provide some guidance for using accelerative practices on a routine basis at all stages of development.

Acceleration policies in schools should ensure that opportunities such as the ones described here are available provisions in all gifted programs for individuals and groups of learners ready to advance beyond the standard curriculum at any age and in any area of learning.

Source: National Association for Gifted Children, 2004, pp. 1–2.

ENRICHMENT TACTICS

Enrichment introduces students to topics and methods of learning not ordinarily available in the standard curriculum. Enrichment tactics can be separated into three subgroups:

1. Tactics that provide students with opportunities to practice and polish skills and content materials that are part of the regular curriculum

2. Tactics that extend knowledge in content areas that students have studied in the regular curriculum

3. Tactics that introduce knowledge and skills that are not part of the regular curriculum

Following are some ways to help students who are gifted and talented enrich what they have learned.

1. **To practice and polish skills in writing, use open activities.** Open activities foster creativity. At a writing center, write the following categories across a sign, poster, or chalkboard. Provide ten items in each category; four examples follow.

Character	Goals	Obstacles	Results
1. Larry Johnson	1. Fame	1. Disability	1. Graduated
2. Bo Jackson	2. Wealth	2. Publicity	2. Quit Yankees
3. Brooke Shields	3. To be athlete	3. Temper	3. Superstar
4. Michael Jackson	4. College degree	4. Competition	4. Famous

Character	Goals	Obstacles	Results
1. Brett Favre			
1. Fame			
1. Disability			
1. Graduated			

2. Michael Jordan
2. Wealth
2. Publicity
2. Quit Yankees
3. Jennifer Lopez
3. To be athlete
3. Temper
3. Superstar
4. Eminem
4. College degree
4. Competition
4. Famous

Provide the following directions on a task card:

Directions for Creative Writing Activity

- Write down your phone number, for example, 555–2214.
- Drop the first three digits, for example, 2214.
- Use the last four digits to match the items in each of the four categories; for example, 2214 would be Michael Jordan, Wealth, Disability, and Famous.
- Write whatever story comes to your mind (fact or fiction) using the items your digits match.

---

2. **To practice and polish skills in mathematics, change the location for learning.** Students at the primary level find facts fun to learn if they must work them out lying on the floor with a flashlight. Have students read facts off the bottom of a table. Older students enjoy taking assignments outside to be completed.

3. **To practice and polish number facts, combine sports and math.** After students have mastered basic math facts, relate them to team and individual statistics. For instance, teach students how to compute batting averages, shooting percentages, or won/loss records, and have them keep statistics for their favorite teams during appropriate seasons.

4. **To practice and polish mathematics performance, use problem-solving games.** Prepare a set of index cards that contain open-ended math problems (see *Figure 3.1*). Challenge students to use the six boxed-numbers once with any math operation (addition, subtraction, multiplication, division) to arrive at a solution as close as possible to the target solution (560). Award points based on proximity to the target solution and have students create their own problems to share with other classes or their classmates.

Figure 3.1   Open-Ended Math Problems

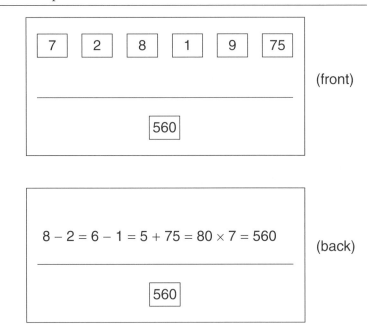

1. **To practice and polish mathematics performance, use surveys and research methods.** Prepare a list of questions that require the use of estimation and inference. Place each question on an index card (see *Figure 3.2*) with space for a prediction, a description of a method(s) that could be used to arrive at a solution, and a solution. Have students work in teams conducting research to answer the questions. Compare and contrast the solutions found by using different methods.

Figure 3.2   Field Research Card

Field Research Card

06–001

Research Question: How many bricks are on the outside structure of the school building?

Prediction:

Method:

Solution:

Sample research questions:

- How many books are in the school library?
- How many students' shoes have laces?
- How close can you get to a bird?
- How many names are in the white pages of our phone book?
- How many pieces of popcorn would fill a file cabinet?
- How many people in school have blond hair?
- How many people in the city live in brick houses?
- How many people in the city drive white cars?
- How many people in school have fall birthdays?
- How many teachers are more than 40 years old?

2. **To extend skills in all academic areas, use free-time activities that apply learning.** For example, a map reading center can be used to extend mathematics and social studies by emphasizing solving problems that involve travel. Have students use maps and atlases to plan trips and/or solve problems such as the following:
   - Find where you live on the map. Make an X with your pencil. Find a place that is 20 miles from your town (e.g., Springfield).
   - Compute the distance to Springfield from where you live. If your car gets 15 miles per each gallon of gas, how many gallons would it take to get to Springfield?

- Find a town that is north of where you live. Circle it with your pencil.
- Find a town that is south of where you live. Draw a line under it.

3. **To extend skills in creative writing, prompt students to use adjectives and adverbs.** Create a center in which students can develop methods of observation: a close-up view, a panorama, looking at something through a pin-hole in a piece of paper, looking through a concave or convex lens. Ask students to describe their observations using adjectives and adverbs. Provide a thesaurus and a dictionary. To vary this activity, have students record their impressions on a tape recorder.

4. **To extend skills in creative writing, use the Internet.** Have students find students in other cities, states, or nations to become pen pals for sharing information about their school and life experiences. Prepare personal information sheets on students' backgrounds and special interests when sending or receiving communications. Have students keep records of cities, states, and nations that are part of their creative writing network.

5. **To extend research skills, use computer data resources.** Have students choose a topic of interest to them and research it on the Internet. As the end product of their research, have students create a computerized multimedia presentation for their classmates or for parent–teacher night.

6. **To extend knowledge in social studies, mix history and the arts.** Illustrate lectures on periods of history with centers depicting artwork from that period. For instance, lessons on American history during the 1920s can be accompanied by an in-depth look at the art of the Works Progress Administration. Encourage students to read about literature, fashion, drama, and architecture from periods of history that are being studied.

7. **To extend knowledge in any content area, increase career awareness.** Invite people who are actively involved in various careers to meet with students, not only to talk

about their professional fields but also to discuss the specialized methods and tools they use to accomplish their work tasks.

8. **To extend knowledge in any content area, encourage students to add to the curriculum.** Have students review curriculum content to identify outdated information and possible new topics.

9. **To extend knowledge in science, use literature.** Many works of literature, particularly science fiction, introduce scientific concepts and discoveries that students can learn about in greater depth. Following is an example of a task card at a learning center designed to follow up on scientific descriptions found in the science fiction story "Zero Hour" by Ray Bradbury (Swan, 1977). The center would be appropriate for students who are gifted and talented in any grade.

"Zero Hour"

Ray Bradbury

In this science fiction story, technology of the future is described. Using the magazines and journals provided (such as *Discovery*, *Science Digest*, and *Smithsonian*), list scientific breakthroughs you believe will affect the world and its population. Choose a few of these breakthroughs and describe how they will affect us. Then group your findings together in categories (e.g., methods of communication, travel, satisfying needs, defense). For instance, travel may be affected by a group of discoveries entitled "time travel" or "solar energy."

---

1. **To extend knowledge into new areas, introduce new topics in the classroom.** Using such magazines as *National Geographic*, *Science Digest*, and *Natural History*, have students who are gifted and talented select a new

topic each month and create a learning center based on a theme.

2. **To extend knowledge into new areas, use human resources.** Create a volunteer, mentor, or community resource file for the class. Have the "human resources" do class presentations describing their professional preparation, activities, and goals. Have them also describe current trends and future needs in their respective areas as a way to introduce students to real-world applications for new knowledge. Have students plan the file, locate resource people, interview them, and develop resource file entries.

3. **To extend knowledge into new areas, use book reporting.** Book reporting can stretch learning beyond the regular curriculum. Have students:
   - Make a list of things that would make their book better.
   - Make a list of the interesting words in the book and tell why they are interesting.
   - Make a list of ten words that tell about the story and then decide which one of the words tells the most.
   - Make a list of three opinions that others might have about the book and the reasons for each opinion.
   - Write alternative endings to the story.
   - Write descriptions about the book from the point of view of their favorite character(s).

4. **To encourage forecasting, use book reporting.** Have students:
   - Predict what someone who reads the book in the future will say about it.
   - Predict what a historical person would have said about the book if that person had read it.
   - Predict what a character in another book would say about the book.
   - Predict what someone older would say about the book.
   - Locate and list cause-and-effect relations in the story.
   - Write what might happen in a second version of the book.

5. **To encourage dramatic talent, use book reporting.** Have students:

- Write or tell how the book is the same as or different from their lives.
- Present a play based on the book.
- Give a class report as they think one of the characters in the book would present it.
- Read the book (or a part of it) to a group of younger students.
- Give a report to the class the way the author of the book would give it.

6. **To encourage artistic talent, use book reporting.** Have students:
   - Draw a series of pictures to retell the sequence of events in the book.
   - Make an original cover for the book.
   - Use crayon, chalk, and paint to illustrate a favorite part of the book.
   - Make a bulletin board display for the book.
   - Make a comic strip of the book.
   - Make a poster to advertise the book.
   - Make a diorama based on the book.
   - Make a mural illustrating the book.

7. **To extend knowledge into new areas, use research to solve real-world problems.** For example, provide task cards such as those in *Figure 3.3*. Have students plan a family vacation or do some catalog shopping as a way to extend what they are learning in math and social studies. Provide all necessary materials for this activity, such as maps, vacation guides, and catalogs.

8. **To extend knowledge into new areas, use drama.** Drama can enrich problem-solving skills. Have students who are gifted and talented list and describe alternative solutions to a problem, the obstacles to those solutions, and the methods needed to remove those obstacles. Next, have them create sociodramas in which a protagonist must develop a plan of action and overcome specific obstacles to implement the plan. Records, videos, filmstrips, books, and other resources can be used to find examples of protagonists who have fought obstacles to solve specific problems.

Figure 3.3

Task Card

Plan a family vacation. Record the dates you plan to travel, where you plan to go, and how you will get there. Calculate the cost of travel, lodging, and other items.

Task Card

Select a wardrobe for a week's vacation. Calculate its cost, including taxes and shipping charges.

ACCELERATION TACTICS

Acceleration involves placing a student in contact with instruction that would normally be encountered at higher grade levels. Acceleration requires structured teacher planning and record keeping to determine those areas of the curriculum in which students show particular strengths. The major arguments against acceleration are that moving students ahead does not help them apply knowledge and that it involves merely presenting material students inevitably will study anyway. Acceleration, such as skipping a grade and concurrent enrollment in high school and college, is usually considered an administrative practice rather than an instructional practice to be implemented by a classroom teacher, but following are some ways to use acceleration with students who are gifted and talented.

1. When giving classroom assignments, have students who are gifted and talented start by completing the most difficult items first or by taking a pretest. Allowing students to complete standard work more quickly reduces the likelihood of boredom and provides opportunities to accelerate individual learning processes. If students demonstrate mastery of the skills being practiced, provide alternative

assignments that introduce more advanced material. For example, if students pass a spelling test with a score of 90 percent or higher, have them bypass regular workbook activities and the end-of-week test by selecting one or more of the following alternative activities:

a. Working with another student who also passed the pretest, find ten new words from other textbooks in the room. Study the words together and give each other a spelling test using the new words.

b. Using weekly spelling words and new words, create the smallest set of sentences that you can using all the words.

c. Create a crossword puzzle and key using the weekly spelling words and new words.

d. Create a set of categories into which all the words will fit.

e. Create a set of greeting-card messages using all the words.

f. Create riddles with the weekly spelling words and new words as answers.

In addition, use diagnostic instruments in the basic skill areas (e.g., reading, language skills, mathematics) to determine which students have mastered grade-level skills and competencies in specific curriculum areas so that more advanced content can be provided.

1. **Develop units or use resources with multiple starting points and multiple activities.** These will allow students to start and continue their work at varying levels according to their abilities, experiences, prior learning, and interests. **Programmed learning**, introduced through commercially designed materials, involves diagnosing students by preestablished instruments and putting them into learning resources at a point at which they demonstrate content mastery. These materials offer skills and objectives prearranged and sequenced on a continuum from simple to complex. Instructional packages are less

Bringing Learning to Life: Instructional Acceleration

Lenny, the first student introduced at the beginning of this book, has won awards in diverse areas and will enter Harvard when he is 16. Professionals in the school system where Lenny lives recognize that special programs require flexibility to accommodate the varying skills, abilities, and interests of students who are gifted and talented. When planning for individual students, they think in terms of combinations of programs rather than single types of programs. Lenny had the following program alternatives available to meet his needs for instructional acceleration:

Cluster grouping: Students with high ability are placed together in one classroom rather than spread among teachers at a grade level.

Interest grouping: Students with similar abilities and interests are provided opportunities to work together during regular school hours.

Multiage classes: Students with similar abilities are taught together in one classroom rather than spread among teachers at different grade levels.

Grade-skipping: Students with high ability are allowed to skip a particular grade and advance to the next.

Telescoping: Students with high ability are placed together in a multiage classroom with the intention of completing two years of work in one academic year.

Acceleration classes: Students with high ability are provided opportunities to enroll in coursework at higher grade levels, at other schools in the system, and at colleges and universities.

During his school career, Lenny skipped several grades, completed third and fourth grade in one year, and always was part of a cluster grouping plan initiated when his superior abilities were first identified. During his last school year, he took advanced calculus at the local university along with other freshman courses.

structured; the students select and explore a variety of materials based on interest, selected goals, self-pacing, and individual leveling. As students use programmed learning or instructional package materials, record the skill they have mastered.

Bringing Learning to Life: Curriculum Compacting Emphasizes Strengths of Gifted Students

In the opening of this book, we told you about Nicholas, whose parents almost enrolled him in a special school. Nicholas's teachers were sympathetic to his feelings of boredom and his passion for writing. They decided to use curriculum compacting as an instructional alternative in his school program. First, they pretested Nicholas in every area of the semester's content. After analyzing his performance, they decided that Nicholas would have an hour a day available for his own work. They arranged for him to use his free time to work on his biography of Eleanor Roosevelt in the library at school.

They also provided opportunities for Nicholas to spend time with upper-grade teachers who were teaching students about biographies as part of their literature programs. They contacted a local author and provided opportunities for the author to review Nicholas's book and discuss ways to improve his writing skills. In explaining the special program to Nicholas's classmates, his teachers stressed the criterion that had to be demonstrated (content mastery) and offered the same opportunities (intensive work on a project of their choice) to all of them. None took advantage of it.

1. **Use advanced tests and curriculum materials.** Obtain sample copies of textbooks and curriculum materials at many levels to provide challenging and appropriate instructional materials in a variety of subjects.

2. **Develop a talent pool in your classroom.** Encourage individual students to become "experts" or "consultants"

on a particular concept, skill, or subject. Have students prepare a "Yellow Pages" directory that advertises their expertise. Provide a mailbox or separate mailboxes in which students can put questions they have written for the experts. Questions and answers can be recorded, if the students wish. During a group free period (such as just before lunch or before leaving school), call on the student experts to share their questions and answers with the class.

3. **Use curriculum compacting to provide opportunities for acceleration experiences.** Allow students to "buy" time for acceleration activities when they have demonstrated competence. For example, if a student obtains a score of 90 percent or better on a writing test, he or she might earn time to work on an independent writing project. If a student demonstrates mastery on a math pretest, he or she might be permitted to buy time to solve problems from advanced placement tests. The key to this form of compacting is identifying specific skills students have mastered and allowing them to complete alternative activities instead of practicing what they already know.

4

What Trends and Issues Influence How We Teach Students With Gifts and Talents?

P ublic schools did not have widespread programs for gifted and talented students before the development of the first intelligence tests. One of the earliest tests to be used in the United States was the Binet-Simon Intelligence Scale (Terman, 1911). In describing usage of this test, Terman (1916) talked about giftedness and gifted people—those who scored in the top 2 percent of the population. Over time, this was operationalized as a score of two standard deviations above average (standard score of 130 or above) on other intelligence tests. Today, most educators say that students who are gifted and talented are those who score above 130 on an intelligence test.

THE EVOLVING CONCEPT OF GIFTEDNESS

In 1972 an effort was made to broaden the concept of giftedness. In a report to Congress, Sidney Marland (1972, p. 10) defined children who are gifted and talented as:

those identified by professionally qualified persons, who, by virtue of outstanding abilities, are capable of high performance. These are children who require differentiated educational programs and services beyond those normally provided by the regular program in order to realize their contribution to self and society. Children capable of high performance include those with demonstrated and/or potential ability in any of the following areas:

1. General intellectual ability

2. Specific academic aptitude

3. Creative or productive thinking

4. Leadership ability

5. Visual and performing arts

Since the early work of Terman, professionals have debated the definition of giftedness and the specific criteria used in assessment of students as gifted. The debates sound very similar to those you will encounter over definitions and criteria used to identify students with disabilities. For example, professionals debate about the criteria for deciding when students do and do not evidence leadership ability, about the standards to be employed in deciding the extent to which a student demonstrates potential ability as an artist or a performer, and about the age at which giftedness can be identified.

MOVING BEYOND INTELLIGENCE TESTS

Debates about assessment and identification inevitably involve considerations of intelligence and its value in identifying students who are gifted and talented. Intelligence test scores have dominated selection and placement practices because they are easily used to set cutoffs and to make decisions about who is gifted (e.g., individuals with intelligence test scores of 130 or higher).

Recently, the concept of intelligence has been extended to represent more than a score on an intelligence test. Arguing that there are at least two types of giftedness—**schoolhouse giftedness,** measured by performance on tests, and **creative-productive giftedness,** evidenced by development of original materials and products—Renzulli (1978, 1979) downplayed the importance of intelligence test scores as primary identification measures.

Robert Sternberg (1985) argued that giftedness had three aspects. The first is cognitive and internal to the individual. The second is experiential, relating thinking to personal experience to solve problems. Third, a gifted individual may be superior in adapting to, shaping, and selecting experiences. For Sternberg and Davidson (1986b), giftedness comes in several varieties:

> Some gifted individuals may be particularly adept at applying the components of intelligence, but only to academic kinds of situations. They may thus be "test-smart," but little more. Other [individuals who are gifted] may be particularly adept at dealing with novelty, but in a synthetic rather than an analytic sense: Their creativity is not matched by analytic power. Still other [individuals who are gifted] may be "street-smart" in external contexts, but at a loss in academic contexts. Thus, giftedness is plural rather than singular in nature. (p. 9)

Howard Gardner (1983) proposed a **multiple intelligences (MI) theory** in which all individuals are capable of at least seven independent forms of intellectual performance: linguistic, musical, logical-mathematical, spatial, bodily-kinesthetic, interpersonal, and intrapersonal. He believed that each could be developed to high levels and that each should be considered in identification efforts.

Nobody really knows what giftedness is, and there are no objective measures of it. This doesn't matter too much when members of society value giftedness as "arguably the most precious natural resource a civilization can have" (Sternberg & Davidson 1986a, p. ix). It causes problems only when groups of people are overlooked as identification practices are implemented.

Underrepresented Groups in the Gifted and Talented Category

The number of girls identified as gifted declines with age, which has caused some professionals to wonder what happens to them (Silverman, 1986, p. 43). One explanation is that behaviors that are valued and measured in gifted identification practices (such as risk-taking, competitiveness, and independence) are not fostered in the socialization of girls. Without them, creativity, achievement, and leadership are limited and girls are overlooked in identification practices.

Stereotypes and other social factors also work against girls. One teacher noticed it with two of her best students in math, Kevin and Chelsea. As part of his special education program, Kevin was "pulled out" for three periods a week with the math specialist. The teacher thought Chelsea should also participate. When the teacher asked her principal about it, the principal said she didn't think girls needed math enrichment because eventually their aptitudes for it were replaced by interests and abilities in areas related to writing, language, and the arts. The teacher pointed out to the principal that women have been successful in greater and greater numbers in professions traditionally pursued by men largely because schools were no longer fostering such stereotypes.

The teacher then talked to other teachers and, with her principal's support, started an afterschool enrichment program for girls who were gifted in math. When giftedness is associated mainly with high scores on intelligence tests or other unitary criteria, people with limited ranges of performance on these measures are at a disadvantage. Communication disorders, differences in native language, physical disabilities, learning disabilities, and emotional disabilities can influence individuals' scores on any test. Because of the limitations of most tests and theories of giftedness, tests have not been particularly helpful in identification of people with disabilities who are gifted and talented.

Some people also slip through the cracks when singular conceptions of intelligence or giftedness are used for identification. Several categories of students are particularly neglected in programs for top students. These include children from some cultures and from families experiencing economic disadvantage, students with high IQs who do not achieve in school, and students with artistic talent (Office of Educational Research and Improvement, 1993; Reichert, 1987; Saccuzzo, Johnson, & Guertin, 1994). For example, in data compiled by the Office of Educational Research and Improvement (1993), only 9 percent of students participating in programs for the gifted and talented were in the bottom 25 percent relative to family income (compared to 47 percent from the top 25 percent), and fewer than expected students from African American, Hispanic, and American Indian families participated.

Schools in some states are discouraged from serving these students by rules and regulations that force them to use specific IQ cutoffs or levels of performance as a basis for identification. Most states encourage the use of test scores because they are easier to determine and "safer" than more subjective and comprehensive measures. Practices based on such principles are often seen as unsatisfactory because of their effects on important, underrepresented groups of students.

TIPS FOR TEACHERS

There are no simple solutions to problems facing those who teach students who are gifted and talented (Gallagher & Coleman, 1992; Reichert, 1987; Reis & Purcell, 1993). If you teach, you will have some of these students in your classroom. You may be challenged to make alternatives work for students sometimes overlooked in traditional efforts to reach students who are gifted and talented. Here are a few tips:

- Use multiple measures of ability when identifying students for gifted and talented programs.
- Hold high expectations in all content areas for all your students.
- Acknowledge the concept of multiple intelligences and strive to support the "expert" in all your students.
- Avoid sexist, cultural, classist, and ethnic stereotypes and discuss them regularly with your students.

- Design career development activities that include successful people from varied groups.
- Expose your students to positive role models from traditional and nontraditional groups.
- Form support groups for students with similar interests.
- Have students read biographies of gifted people from traditionally underrepresented groups.

5

Gifts and Talents in Perspective

In general, teachers of students who are gifted and talented must pay attention to the pace at which these students learn, the depth at which they are allowed to explore topics, and the extent to which the students' own interests are incorporated into lessons and learning activities. There is no magic in implementing these effective teaching practices. Everything written about teaching students who are gifted and talented stresses the importance of modifying the curricular content beyond presentation of simple facts, rules, and details to identification of complex generalizations, issues, and solutions to problems. Classroom teachers of students who are gifted and talented generally gain time for extension activities by modifying regular classroom assignments, involving students in independent or group activities, and structuring assignments to allow content enrichment. Their hope is the same as that of other teachers—that their efforts will enable their students to lead productive and valuable lives.

A climate of educational reform has engulfed America's schools. Calls for richer and deeper experiences for students are seen as ways to combat our loss of economic competitiveness in the world. New organizational structures are placing teachers and schools under increasing pressure to produce outcomes and bolster evidence of accountability. More and more children are coming to school from diverse ethnic and linguistic backgrounds, forcing teachers to place more importance on the context of their work than ever before in history (Ogbu, 1992). This climate of interest and action will have a positive effect on educational programs for the nation's most talented students if communities value intellectual and artistic accomplishment and support schools and teachers in fostering it. For community-wide support to occur, education professionals need to provide direction for serious educational reform (Office of Educational Research and Improvement, 1993).

First, challenging curriculum standards must be established, and the responsibility for challenging students to achieve them must be shared by teachers and other members of society. As state and local education agencies develop standards for student performance, they must ensure that ceilings for performance are raised for students who are capable of the highest levels of achievement.

Second, opportunities that meet the needs of students who are gifted and talented must be available. These experiences must be provided inside and outside of school buildings and be diverse enough to accommodate the varied skills and talents of these students. Providing in-depth work to extend knowledge in core curriculum areas, accelerating the rate at which the core curriculum is presented and mastered, enrolling in special classes that enhance interests in specific areas, and providing work experiences within the local community are examples of how new opportunities will be provided.

Third, teachers, parents, and other professionals must look for strengths and potential in younger and younger children. Schools and community agencies must work with parents to help them learn, and provide parents with ways to nurture their children and help them achieve in school. Schools need to extend their spheres of influence to preschool programs in the community; such efforts should be directed at ensuring that strengths identified in preschool are extended into elementary, middle, and high school programs.

Fourth, opportunities for children from diverse cultures and from families experiencing economic disadvantage must be expanded. Barriers to achievement that are common for many of these children must be overcome. Hindrances to participation in programs for students who are gifted and talented that are currently experienced by many of these children must be eliminated.

Finally, schools of the future must adopt a vision that fosters a richer curriculum for all students, supports each student's potential, and encourages teachers to develop their own talents and those of every student. Toward this goal, the following perspective on "excellent schools" describes what education for all students should be (Office of Educational Research and Improvement, 1993, p. 29):

> All children progress through challenging material at their own pace. Students are grouped and regrouped based on their interests and needs. Achieving success for all students is not equated with achieving the same results for all students.
>
> Diversity is honored in students' backgrounds as well as in their abilities and interests. The classroom, school organization, and instructional strategies are designed to accommodate [and value] diversity and to find strengths in all children.
>
> Students know that parents, educators, and other important adults in their lives set high expectations for them and watch them closely to ensure that they work to their ability and develop their potential. The community provides the resources needed to adapt and enrich the curriculum to meet student needs. School faculty and administrators ensure that community and school resources are matched with students' strengths and needs.
>
> Students gain self-esteem and self-confidence from mastering work that initially seemed slightly beyond their grasp.
>
> Students emerge from their education eager to learn and confident that they can join the intellectual, cultural, and work life of the nation.

Everybody wins in such schools. All students have similar opportunities for developing skills and demonstrating performance. All teachers are expected to nurture and support learning, and they are rewarded for doing so. All parents see growth in their children as a result of the teaching and learning that goes on in their schools. That's the way education should be, and society would benefit from it.

6

What Have We Learned?

As you complete your study of teaching students with gifts and talents, it may be helpful to review what you have learned. To help you check your understanding, we have listed the key points and key vocabulary for you to review. We have included the Self-Assessment again so you can compare what you know now with what you knew as you began your study. Finally, we provide a few topics for you to think about and some activities for you to do "on your own."

KEY POINTS

▣ Students who are gifted and talented are known more for their contributions and potential contributions than any other group of students.

▣ Terms used to refer to students who are gifted and talented are generally favorable, but these students may also experience problems in school, such as boredom, alienation from peers, and pressures to do well in all areas of performance.

- A variety of characteristics have been identified in students who are gifted and talented. Most reflect outstanding performance in cognitive, academic, behavioral, or related areas.

- For many students, giftedness does not extend across all school subject areas.

- Successful teaching approaches usually emphasize the attainment of higher levels of understanding, not just greater repetition of facts.

- Two primary types of instructional approaches—enrichment and acceleration—are used by teachers and other professionals to help these students be successful in school and later life.

- Continuing concerns for teachers and other professionals working with students who are gifted and talented are identification, cultural diversity, and the inclusion of populations that have been underrepresented in the past. Teaching students who are gifted and talented means being aware of these problems and their potentially detrimental effects on special education programs.

Key Vocabulary

Acceleration or **advancement** refers to double promotion, skipping grades, or advanced enrollment in higher-level coursework.

Convergent thinking is reflected on measures of reasoning ability, memory, and classification.

Creative-productive giftedness is evidenced by development of original materials and products.

Divergent thinking is characterized by creativity, fluency, flexibility, originality, and foresight.

Enrichment is used when teachers provide experiences or activities that are beyond the standard curriculum.

Gifted is usually used to refer to people with superior intellectual or cognitive performance.

Multiple intelligences refers to the theory in which all individuals are capable of at least seven independent forms of intellectual performance: linguistic, musical, logical-mathematical, spatial, bodily-kinesthetic, interpersonal, and intrapersonal.

Programmed learning means diagnosing students using preestablished instruments and putting them into learning resources at a point at which they demonstrate content mastery.

Schoolhouse giftedness is thought to be measured by performance on tests.

Talented is usually used to refer to people who show outstanding performance in a specific area such as the performing or visual arts.

Self-Assessment 2

After you complete this book, check your knowledge and understanding of the content covered. Choose the best answer for each of the following questions.

1. A term used to refer to people with superior intellectual or cognitive abilities is:

   a. Exceptional

   b. Gifted

   c. Talented

   d. Advanced

2. The term that describes people who show outstanding performance in a specific area such as the performing or visual arts is:

   a. Phenomenal

   b. Gifted

   c. Talented

   d. Outstanding

3. Legislation that provides states financial incentive to develop programs for students who are gifted and talented is:

   a. P. L. 99–457

   b. P. L. 94–142

   c. P. L. 95–561

   d. P. L. 95–142

4. What percentage of the total school-age population is estimated to be gifted and/or talented?

   a. 1–3 percent

   b. 3–5 percent

   c. 5–10 percent

   d. 10–15 percent

5. Regarding state legislation for educational programs for students who are gifted and talented:

   a. Educational services are provided in very few states.

   b. Educational services are left up to the discretion of local school districts.

   c. Educational services are mandated in all states.

   d. Educational services are mandated in some states.

6. Common cognitive traits associated with giftedness are:

   a. Rapid generalization, slow comprehension of abstract concepts

   b. Rapid generalization, poor memory

   c. Diminished comprehension of simple relationships

   d. Rapid generalization, quick comprehension of abstract concepts

7. Students who perform well on measures of _____ thinking are usually thought of as creative individuals.

   a. Convergent

   b. Abstract

   c. Complex

   d. Divergent

8. Students who perform well on measures of _____ thinking are thought to show academic aptitude.

   a. Convergent

   b. Abstract

   c. Complex

   d. Divergent

9. Thinking that involves reasoning ability, memory, and classification is:

   a. Convergent

   b. Abstract

   c. Complex

   d. Divergent

10. Individuals who have the skill of flexible thinking are able to:

   a. Produce many words, a variety of associations, phrases, and sentences

   b. Offer a variety of ideas and alternate solutions to problems

   c. Use rare responses and unique words

   d. See alternative solutions ahead of time

REFLECTION

After you answer the multiple-choice questions, think about how you would answer the following questions:

- What factors might affect the academic success of individuals with gifts and talents?

- What differentiates individuals with gifts and talents from other exceptional people?
- What do effective teachers do to provide support for students with gifts and talents?

Answer Key for Self-Assessments

1. b

2. c

3. c

4. b

5. d

6. d

7. d

8. a

9. a

10. b

On Your Own

☑ Imagine that you are a teacher with several students who are gifted and talented in your classroom. What decisions would you make to help these students be successful? What instructional approaches would be appropriate? What specific activities would you use to enrich a lesson you were teaching to your class on dinosaurs?

☑ Attend a parents' group that is concerned with education of students who are gifted and talented. List the topics that are discussed. Interview at least three parents to obtain their overall impressions of the services provided by the school system to their children.

☑ Write a brief paper explaining what you know about teaching students who are gifted and talented. Include the following information: definition, characteristics, prevalence, and interventions that could be used in any classroom to improve the educational program being provided.

☑ Pick a topic that would be appropriate to teach a group of elementary, middle, or high school students. Plan an instructional presentation that you could use to teach basic content and extend students' knowledge and thinking skills related to the topic.

☑ Think about two people who you think are gifted and talented. List five different characteristics for each person that supports your opinion that they are gifted and talented. List five characteristics that illustrate similarities between these two people.

☑ Review the names of Gardner's seven multiple intelligences. Think of ways you would identify students exhibiting one type and not the others. Think of people you know who have developed high levels of performance in one of the areas but not others. Write down your impressions of this theory and share them with a friend.

Resources

BOOKS

Baldwin, A. (2004). *Culturally diverse and underserved populations of gifted students.* Thousand Oaks, CA: Corwin. A set of chapters and readings on major issues in, and common strategies for, educating gifted children from diverse populations.

Clark, B. (2002). *Growing up gifted: Developing the potential of children at home and at school.* Englewood Cliffs, NJ: Prentice Hall. This book provides an overview of education considerations for students who are gifted and talented, including identification and programming in elementary and secondary schools, and a chapter on areas of concern in gifted education.

Davis, G. A., & Rimm, S. B. (2004). *Education of the gifted and talented* (5th ed.). Upper Saddle River, NJ: Allyn & Bacon. A comprehensive textbook including specific strategies on educating gifted and talented students.

Gallagher, J. (Ed.). (2004). *Public policy in gifted education.* Thousand Oaks, CA: Corwin. An analytic discussion of critical issues affecting educational reform efforts for gifted and talented students.

Kerr, B. A. (1985). *Smart girls, gifted women.* Columbus: Ohio Psychological Publishing. This collection of case studies offers information about an often underrepresented group of students who are gifted and talented.

Winebrenner, S. (2003). *Teaching gifted kids in regular classes: Strategies and techniques every teacher can use to meet the academic needs of the gifted and talented.* New York: Free Spirit Press.

JOURNALS

Gifted Child Quarterly (GCQ). This publication of the National Association for Gifted Children provides articles that describe research-based program evaluations, program descriptions, and other research-oriented activities. Articles further the knowledge base and improve the lives of people who are gifted and talented. Gifted Child Quarterly, 5100 N. Edgewood Dr., St. Paul, MN 55112.

Journal for the Education of the Gifted (JEG). JEG is a publication of the Council for Exceptional Children's Association for the Gifted. Its provides a forum for current research related to individuals who are gifted and talented and provides information about teacher training and programming. Articles further the knowledge base and improve service to individuals who are gifted and talented. James J. Gallagher, Editor, University of North Carolina, 300 Nations Bank Plaza, Chapel Hill, NC 27514.

Roeper Review (RR). RR focuses on practical suggestions for improving programs for the gifted and talented. Occasionally this journal publishes thematic issues in which all the articles address a central topic such as assessment or cultural diversity in gifted and talented education. Roeper City and County Schools, 2190 N. Woodward, Bloomfield Hills, MI 48013.

ORGANIZATIONS

American Association for Gifted Children (AAGC)

This advocacy group supports families, children, and educational programs. It promotes awareness and supportive activities for people who are gifted and talented. AAGC, 15 Gramercy Park, New York, NY 10003.

The Association for the Gifted (TAG)

A division of the Council for Exceptional Children, TAG encourages membership of professionals interested in program development and preparation activities related to educating individuals who are gifted and talented. TAG provides outlets for the exchange of ideas through a variety of resources, including the *Journal for the Education of the Gifted*. CEC, 1100 N. Glebe Road, Suite 300, Arlington, VA 22201–5704.

National Association for Gifted Children (NAGC)

Membership in NAGC includes parents, teachers, and professionals interested in programs for people who are gifted and talented. With *Gifted Child Quarterly* and other resources, NAGC is a primary agency for information, materials, guidance, and networking advice. NAGC, 5100 N. Edgewood Dr., St. Paul, MN 55112.

References

Education for All Handicapped Children Act, Pub. L. No. 94–142, 89 Stat. 773 (1975).

Gallagher, J. (1985). *Teaching the gifted child* (3rd ed.). Boston: Allyn & Bacon.

Gallagher, J., & Coleman, M. R. (1992). *State policies on the identification of gifted students from special populations: Three states in profile.* Chapel Hill, NC: Gifted Education Policy Studies Program.

Gallagher, J., & Gallagher, S. (1994). *Teaching the gifted child* (4th ed.). Boston: Allyn & Bacon.

Gardner, H. (1983). *Frames of mind.* New York: Basic Books.

Gardner, H. (1993). *Frames of mind* (10th anniversary edition). New York: Basic Books.

Gifted and Talented Children's Education Act, Pub. L. No. 95–561 (1978).

Individuals With Disabilities Education Act, Pub. L. No. 101–476, 104 Stat. 1141 (1990).

Jakob K. Javits Gifted and Talented Students Act, Pub. L. No. 100–297 (1988).

Larsen, M. D., Griffin, N. S., & Larsen, L. M. (1994). Public opinion regarding support for special programs for gifted children. *Journal for the Education of the Gifted, 17,* 131–142.

Louisiana Department of Education. (2000). Regulations for implementation of the Children With Exceptionalities Act (R.S. 17:1941 et seq.): Bulletin 1706 Subpart B–Regulations for gifted/talented students. Baton Rouge, LA: Author.

Marland, S. (1972). *1971 Report to Congress of the U.S. Department of Education.* Washington, DC: U.S. Government Printing Office.

Maryland Department of Education. (2001). *Facts 45: Gifted and talented education.* Baltimore, MD: Author.

Minnesota State Advisory Council for the Gifted and Talented. (1988, April 22). *Minnesota standards for services to gifted and talented students.* St. Paul: Author.

National Association for Gifted Children. (2004). *Acceleration* (Position paper). Washington, DC: Author.

Office of Educational Research and Improvement. (1993). *National excellence: A case for developing America's talent.* Washington, DC: U.S. Department of Education.

Ogbu, J. U. (1992). Understanding cultural diversity. *Educational Researcher, 21*(8), 5–14.

Reichert, E. S. (1987). Rampant problems and promising practices in the identification of disadvantaged students. *Gifted Child Quarterly, 31,* 149–154.

Reis, S. M., & Purcell, J. H. (1993). An analysis of content elimination and strategies used by elementary teachers in the curriculum compacting process. *Journal for the Education of the Gifted, 16,* 147–170.

Renzulli, J. (1978). What makes giftedness? Reexamining a definition. *Phi Delta Kappan, 60,* 180–184.

Renzulli, J. (1979). *What makes giftedness? A reexamination of the definition of the gifted and talented* (Brief No. 6). Los Angeles: National/State Leadership Training Institute of the Gifted and Talented.

Saccuzzo, D. P., Johnson, N. E., & Guertin, T. L. (1994). *Identifying underrepresented disadvantaged gifted and talented children: A multifaceted approach* (Vol. 1). San Diego, CA: San Diego State University.

Silverman, L. K. (1986). What happens to the gifted girl? In C. J. Maker (Ed.), *Critical issues in gifted education: Vol. 1. Defensible programs for the gifted* (pp. 43–89). Austin, TX: Pro-Ed.

Sternberg, R. J. (1985). *Beyond IQ: A triarchic theory of human intelligence.* Cambridge, UK: Cambridge University Press.

Sternberg, R. J., & Davidson, J. E. (Eds.). (1986a). *Conceptions of giftedness.* Cambridge, UK: Cambridge University Press.

Sternberg, R. J., & Davidson, J. E. (1986b). Conceptions of giftedness: A map of the terrain. In R. J. Sternberg & J. E. Davidson (Eds.), *Conceptions of giftedness* (pp. 3–18). Cambridge, UK: Cambridge University Press.

Sternberg, R. J., & Davidson, J. E. (Eds.). (2005). *Conceptions of giftedness* (2nd ed.). Cambridge, UK: Cambridge University Press.

Swan, M. (Ed.). (1977). *Zero hour and other modern stories.* London: Cambridge University Press.

Terman, L. (1911). The Binet-Simon Scale for measuring intelligence: Impressions gained by its application. *Psychological Clinic, 5,* 199–206.

Terman, L. (1916). *The measurement of intelligence.* Boston: Houghton Mifflin.

Terman, L., & Oden, M. (1951). The Stanford studies of the gifted. In P. Witty (Ed.), *The gifted child.* Boston: Heath.

Index

Note: Numbers in **Bold** followed by a colon [:] denote the book number within which the page numbers are found.

AAMR (American Association on Mental Retardation), **12:**6, **12:**20–21, **12:**66
Ability training, **4:**39–40, **4:**62
Academic achievement, assessing, **3:**37–39
 achievement tests, **3:**37, **3:**77
 interviews, **3:**38–39
 observations, **3:**38
 portfolios, **3:**39
Academic engaged time, **3:**22–23, **3:**76
Academic learning disabilities, **9:**51
Academic time analysis, **3:**22–23, **3:**76
Acceleration or advancement, **13:**25–27, **13:**36–40, **13:**52
Acceptability, **3:**56–57
Accommodations
 defining, **3:**77
 for student with sensory disabilities, **7:**49–51
 in general education classrooms, **1:**21–22
 without patronization, **4:**14
 See also Instruction, adapting for students with special needs

Accountability, **3:**17, **3:**77
 outcomes-based, **3:**23, **6:**35
Acculturation, **3:**63, **3:**77
Achievement tests, **3:**37, **3:**77
Acting out, **3:**47
Active observation, **3:**29, **3:**77
Adams, C. M., **1:**35–36
Adaptive behavior, **3:**41–43, **3:**77
 defining, **12:**21
 environmental effects on, **3:**42–43
 mental retardation and, **12:**17, **12:**19–25, **12:**21 (tab)–23 (tab), **12:**45–49
Adaptive behavior scales, **3:**42, **12:**71
Adaptive devices, **8:**52, **8:**62–63
ADHD. *See* Attention deficit hyperactivity disorder
Adult literacy/lifelong learning, **5:**50, **6:**27–28
Advanced Placement (AP), **13:**26
Advocacy groups, **6:**11, **6:**12–13, **6:**44
Ahlgren, C., **12:**67
AIDS, **5:**10, **8:**12–13, **8:**58–59, **8:**63
Aim line, **4:**29, **4:**63
Alcohol-/drug-free schools, **6:**28–29
Algozzine, B., **4:**5, **6:**9, **12:**62
Alley, G., **4:**45

Allocation of funds,
6:15, 6:16–17, 6:44
Allsop, J., 8:49
Alternative living unit (ALU),
5:31, 5:54
Alternative-print format, 3:71
Alternatives for recording
answers, 3:71
Amendments to the Education for
All Handicapped Children Act,
2:11 (tab)
Amendments to the Individuals
With Disabilities Education
Act, 2:12 (tab), 2:27–29
American Association on Mental
Retardation (AAMR),
12:6, 12:11, 12:18–19,
12:20–21, 12:66
American Asylum for the
Education and Instruction
of the Deaf, 2:9–10
American Federation
of Teachers, 6:11
American Psychiatric
Association, 9:44
American Sign Language (ASL),
7:40, 7:59
American Speech-Language-
Hearing Association
(ASHA), 10:10, 10:35
Americans With Disabilities
Act (ADA), 2:12 (tab),
2:26–27, 2:54, 8:49
Amplification systems, 4:51, 7:41
Analysis error, 3:38, 3:78
Analytical programs, 9:27, 9:56
Antia, S. D., 7:26
Anxiety, 11:18–22, 11:46
AP (Advanced Placement), 13:26
Apprenticeships programs,
5:45, 5:56
Appropriate education,
2:42 (tab), 2:46, 2:54
ARC (Association for Retarded
Citizens), 12:66
Architectural accessibility, 2:14, 2:54
Articulation disorder,
10:9–10, 10:43

Asch, A., 7:33–34
ASHA (American
Speech-Language-Hearing
Association), 10:10, 10:35
Assessment
academic achievement, 3:37–39
alternatives for recording
answers, 3:71
classroom, 3:73–74
curriculum-based,
3:19–21, 3:78, 9:19
data collection for, 3:25–31
defining, 3:77
ecobehavioral, 3:22–23, 3:78
effects of, 3:74
error and, 3:62–63
formal, 3:11
functional academic,
9:19, 9:57
functional behavioral, 9:19, 9:57,
11:15–16, 11:47
instructional environments,
3:23, 3:77
needs, 4:41, 4:64
portfolios, 3:26, 3:39, 3:80
prereferral interventions, 3:11
psychoeducational, 3:9, 3:81
psychological development,
3:45–47
skilled examiner for, 3:59–61
work-sample, 3:26, 3:81
See also Assessment guidelines;
Assessment practices; Data
collection; Protection in
evaluation procedures
Assessment,
decision-making and
accountability, 3:17
child-study team role in, 3:12–15
eligibility/entitlement, 3:14–15
exceptionality decisions, 3:12
instructional planning, 3:15
intervention assistance, 3:10
overview of, 3:8 (tab)
program evaluation, 3:16–17
progress evaluation, 3:15–16
psychoeducational assessment
referral, 3:9

screening decisions, **3:**7–10
special help/enrichment, **3:**10
special learning needs, **3:**13–14
Assessment guidelines, **3:**65–71
accommodation, **3:**71
environment, **3:**70–71
frequency, **3:**69
improving instruction, **3:**69
more than describing
problems, **3:**67–69
no one cause of school
problems, **3:**66
no right way to assess, **3:**66
variables, **3:**70
Assessment practices, **3:**17–24
curriculum-based assessment,
3:19–21
curriculum-based measurement,
3:21–22
instructional diagnosis, **3:**22
instructional
environments, **3:**23
outcomes-based accountability,
3:23
performance assessment, **3:**24
See also Reliability;
Representativeness; Validity
Assisted listening devices,
7:39 (tab), **7:**41, **7:**42
Assistive technologies,
2:26, **7:**13, **7:**52
Association for Retarded Citizens
(ARC), **12:**66
Asthma, **8:**9–10, **8:**11 (tab), **8:**63
Astigmatism, **7:**10, **7:**59
At risk student, **2:**24, **3:**8, **3:**9,
5:14–15, **6:**20, **13:**14
Ataxic cerebral palsy, **8:**24
Athetoid cerebral palsy, **8:**24
Attack strategy training,
4:40, **4:**63
Attention deficit
hyperactivity disorder
(ADHD), **2:**15, **8:**34
criteria for, **9:**44 (tab)–45 (tab)
defining, **9:**43–46, **9:**56
remediating, **9:**46–48
Audio aids, **7:**36 (tab)

Audiometer, **3:**40, **3:**77
Auditory acuity, **7:**19, **7:**59
Autism, **1:**15–16, **1:**40, **8:**17,
8:28–31, **8:**63
Automaticity, **4:**20, **4:**63
Auxiliary aids, **2:**14

Bain, J. D., **4:**5
Barnett, S., **5:**16
Barraga, N. C., **7:**8
Basic skills, **9:**56
Batshaw, M. L., **8:**22, **8:**47
Beattie v. State Board of Education,
2:36 (tab)
Behavior intervention plan, **11:**16,
11:46
Behavior therapy, **4:**38, **4:**63
Bennett, T., **3:**21
Berdine, W. H., **8:**46
Berrueta-Clement, J., **5:**16
Biklen, D., **6:**41
Bingo (game), **12:**40 (fig)
Blackhurst, A. E., **8:**46
Blackorby, J., **5:**24
Bland, L. C., **1:**35–36
Blindisms, **7:**14
Blindness, **1:**16
defining, **1:**40, **7:**8–9, **7:**59
See also Braille; Visual
impairments
Bloom, B., **4:**41
Books (resources)
assessment, **3:**91–92
communication
disorders, **10:**57
effective instruction, **4:**75–76
emotional disturbance, **11:**57–60
fundamentals of special
education, **1:**53
gifted and talented child,
13:63–64
learning disabilities, **9:**67
legal foundations, **2:**65–66
medical/physical/multiple
disabilities, **8:**75–80
mental retardation, **12:**81–84
public policy/school
reform, **6:**55

sensory disabilities, 7:73–77
transitions, 5:65–67
Bounty hunting, 6:17
Braille, 4:52, 7:10, 7:13, 7:15, 7:16,
7:34, 7:35 (tab)
Braille display technology,
7:37, 7:59
Braille note-taking devices, 7:38
Braille printers, 7:37, 7:59
Brailler, 4:52, 4:63
Brooks-Gunn, J., 5:15
Brophy, J., 4:13
Brown, F., 3:62–63
Brown, L., 12:55, 12:67
Brown v. Board of Education,
2:35, 2:36 (tab), 2:44
Bryant, B., 3:37
Bureau of Indian Affairs,
6:11, 6:13
Burlington School Committee
v. Massachusetts Board of
Education, 2:42 (tab), 2:46–47
Byrnes, L. J., 7:26

Callahan, C. M., 1:35–36
Cameto, R., 5:24
Cancer, 8:11 (tab), 8:63
Canes, for students with visual
impairments, 4:55
Carrow-Woolfolk, E., 10:26
Carta, J., 3:22, 4:46
Carter, K., 7:38
Cartwright, C., 4:53
Cartwright, G., 4:53
Case, L. P., 9:17–18
Categorical programs,
1:17, 6:16, 6:44
CCTV (closed-circuit television),
7:35 (tab), 7:36–37
CEC (Council for Exceptional
Children), 12:66
Cefalu v. East Baton Rouge
Parish School Board,
2:43 (tab)–44 (tab)
Center-based programs,
5:13, 5:14, 5:54
Cerebral palsy, 8:23–24, 8:63
CHADD, 9:46

Chadsey-Rusch, J., 5:24
Chalfant, J. C., 9:51
Chang, S. C., 7:15
Child-find programs,
7:30, 7:59
Child-study team, 3:12–15, 3:77
Choate, J., 3:21
Christenson, S. L., 3:14, 3:23
Citizens Concerned About
Disability, 6:11
Civil Rights Act, 2:26
Clark, B., 4:41
Classification
changes in practices, 6:8–9
defining, 6:44
Classroom amplification systems,
7:41, 7:51
Classroom assessment, 3:73–74
Classwide peer tutoring,
4:47, 4:63
Client-centered therapy,
4:43–44, 4:63
Cloninger, C., 12:59
Close-captioned television, 4:51
Closed-circuit television (CCTV),
7:35 (tab), 7:36–37
Coefficient, reliability, 3:50, 3:81
Cognitive behavior modification,
4:41, 4:63
Cognitive mapping, 7:34
Cognitive skills training,
4:41, 4:43
Cohen, H. J., 8:13
Coleman, M. C., 11:36
Coleman, M. R., 13:11, 13:45
Committee for Economic
Development, 5:14–15
Communication boards,
4:50, 8:41, 8:63
Communication disorders
academic characteristics
of, 10:14
behavioral characteristics
of, 10:15
cognitive characteristics
of, 10:13–14
combating negative stereotypes
about, 10:37 (tab)–38

communication characteristics
    of, **10**:15–16
defining, **10**:43
fluency problems, **10**:16
identifying, **10**:24–27
language disorders, **10**:10–11
language problems, **10**:16
phonology/morphology/
    syntax problems, **10**:10–11
physical characteristics of,
    10:14–15
pragmatics problems, **10**:11
pulling students from classroom,
    10:36–37
semantics problems, **10**:11
speech disorders, **10**:9–10
team approach to providing
    services, **10**:35–36
tips to improve communication,
    10:38
voice problems, **10**:15
See also Communication
    disorders, teaching
    students with
Communication disorders, teaching
    students with, **10**:17–30
interpersonal problems, **10**:27–30
language problems, **10**:20–27
speech problems, **10**:18–20
tips for teachers, **10**:19 (tab)
trends/issues influencing,
    10:31–33
Communication skills, **3**:42
Communication/motility. *See*
    Instructional adaptations, to
    increase
Community collaboration,
    5:7, **5**:43–46, **5**:55, **13**:48
Compensatory education,
    3:10, **3**:77
Competitive employment,
    5:24–25, **5**:55
Computer-assisted
    instruction, **4**:5
Concentration game, **12**:41 (fig)
Concussion, **8**:25–26, **8**:63
Conductive hearing loss,
    7:19, **7**:59

Conlon, C. J., **8**:14
Consultative (indirect) services,
    1:26, **1**:40, **1**:41, **5**:12, **5**:55
Contextual variables, **4**:10, **4**:63
Continued education, **5**:26–27
Contusions, **8**:26, **8**:63
Convergent thinking,
    13:17–18, **13**:52
Cooperative learning,
    4:45–46, **4**:63
Corn, A., **7**:15
Corrective/supportive feedback,
    4:40, **4**:46–47, **12**:37, **12**:43
Council for Children With
    Behavioral Disorders, **11**:36
Council for Exceptional Children
    (CEC), **12**:66
Counseling therapy,
    4:43–45, **4**:63
*Covarrubias v. San Diego Unified
    School District*, **2**:38 (tab)
Craniofacial anomalies,
    8:22, **8**:63
Creative ability, **1**:34, **1**:40–41
Creative-productive giftedness,
    13:43, **13**:52
Creech, B., **7**:26, **7**:42
Crisis therapy, **4**:44–45, **4**:63
Criterion-referenced tests, **3**:28–29,
    3:77–78, **4**:9, **4**:64
Critical thinking, **4**:43
Crittenden, J. B., **7**:87
Crocker, A. C., **8**:13
Cued speech, **7**:39 (tab),
    7:40–41, **7**:42
Cues
    auditory, **7**:16, **7**:28, **7**:43
    defining, **9**:56
    phonetic, **9**:29, **9**:57
    to improve math, **9**:32
    to improve work
        habits, **9**:36
    to reduce behavior problems,
        10:37, **11**:24
Curriculum compacting,
    13:39, **13**:40
Curriculum-based assessment,
    3:19–21, **3**:78, **9**:19

Curriculum-based measurement,
    3:21–22, 3:78
Curriculum-referenced tests. See
    Criterion-referenced tests
Currie, J., 5:15
Cystic fibrosis, 8:12, 8:63

D'Allura, T., 7:14
D'Amico, R., 5:24
Data collection, for assessments,
    3:25–31
Davidson, J. E., 13:43
Davis, L., 12:67
Deaf
    defining, 7:18, 7:21, 7:59
    See also Deaf-and-blind/
        deaf-blind; Hearing
        impairments
Deaf culture, 7:26, 7:59
Deaf-and-blind/deaf-blind
    characteristics of, 7:31–32
    defining, 7:29–30, 7:59–60
    prevalence of, 7:30
Deafness and blindness,
    1:16, 1:41, 7:6, 7:60
Deafness or hearing impairment,
    1:16, 1:41
Deinstitutionalization,
    5:30, 5:55
Delquadri, J., 4:46
Dennis, R., 12:59
Deno, S. L., 3:22
Denton, P., 4:45
Deshler, D., 4:45
Developmental learning
    disabilities, 9:51
Diabetes, 8:11 (tab), 8:63
Diagnostic tests, 3:28, 3:78
Diana v. State Board of
    Education, 2:37 (tab)
Direct instruction,
    principles of, 4:64
    corrective/supportive feedback,
        4:40, 4:46–47, 12:37, 12:43
    independent practice,
        4:40, 10:36–37
    modeling expected
        behavior, 4:40

task analysis, 3:22, 3:81,
    4:10, 4:40, 4:65,
    12:43–45, 12:72
    See also Instruction
Direct services, 1:25, 1:41, 5:12, 5:55
Discrepancy
    defining, 9:56
    dual, 9:17–18
    eliminating, 9:9
Discrepant scores, 3:34, 3:78, 12:30
Discrimination, protection
    against, 1:13
Distractibility (nonattention),
    3:47, 11:47
Disturbed peer relations, 3:47
Divergent thinking, 13:17, 13:52
Diverse students, 1:29–31
Doorlag, D. H., 10:18–20
Down syndrome, 12:13–14,
    12:66, 12:71
Drop out rate, 1:30–31
Drug addiction, pregnancy
    and, 5:10, 8:14–15
DSM-IV, 9:45 (tab)
Dual discrepancy, 9:17–18
Due process, 1:13, 1:41, 2:21,
    2:54, 2:55
Duhaime, A., 8:25, 8:26, 8:27
Dunn, Leota M., 10:27
Dunn, Lloyd M., 10:27
Duration recording, 3:46, 3:78

Early intervention
    as part of lifelong
        learning, 5:50
    defining, 2:55, 5:55, 6:44
    direct/indirect services for, 5:12
    effectiveness of, 5:14–16
    federal laws/incentives
        for, 5:11–12
    for infants/toddlers, 2:24
    Head Start, 5:15
    home-based programs, 5:12–13
    hospital-/center-based programs,
        5:13–14
    need for more programs, 5:10
    preschool, 5:9–10
    social factor influence on, 6:9–10

special education services,
    5:10–11 (fig)
Ypsilanti Perry Preschool
    Project, **5:**15–16
E-books, **9:**29
Echolalia, **8:**41, **11:**14
Ecobehavioral assessment,
    3:22–23, **3:**78
Edelman, S., **12:**59
Education, defining, **1:**9, **1:**41
Education for All Handicapped
    Children Act, **1:**12;
    2:11 (tab), **1:**19
    amendments to, **2:**24–25, **2:**48–49
    defining, **2:**56
    early childhood education and,
        5:11–12
    objectives of, **2:**15
    problems addressed by, **2:**15–16
    provisions of
        (*See* Individualized
        education programs; Least
        restrictive environment;
        Protection in evaluation
        procedures)
    specific learning disabilities and,
        9:11–12
    specific procedures of, **2:**16
    See also Individuals With
        Disabilities Education Act
Educational settings
    diverse, **1:**31–32
    variations by state, **1:**32
    See also Least restrictive
        environment
Egel, A. L., **8:**30
Ekwall, E., **3:**38
Electronic travel aids, **4:**55–56, **4:**64
Elementary and Secondary
    Education Act (ESEA). *See*
    No Child Left Behind Act
Eligibility decisions, **1:**22, **3:**14–15,
    3:78, **7:**9–10, **7:**55
Elliott, J., **4:**5
Emotional disturbance
    academic characteristics of,
        11:10–11
    anxiety, **11:**18–22

behavior intervention plans,
    11:15–16
behavioral characteristics of,
    11:12–14
cognitive characteristics of,
    11:9–10
communication characteristics
    of, **11:**14
defining, **1:**16, **1:**41, **11:**7–9,
    11:35–37, **11:**39–40
functional behavioral assessment
    and, **11:**15–16
improving social interactions,
    11:13–14
medical treatment for, **11:**37–38
physical characteristics of,
    11:11–12
psychosomatic, **11:**11
terms used to describe,
    11:10 (tab)
See also Emotional disturbance,
    teaching students with
Emotional disturbance, teaching
    students with
    anxiety, **11:**18–22
    behavior intervention plans,
        11:17–26
    disruptiveness, **11:**27–29
    nonattention (distractibility),
        11:29–30
    school opposition/
        noncompliance, **11:**23 (tab)
    social problems, **11:**27–33
    task avoidance, **11:**31–33
    temper tantrums, **11:**24–26
    tips for school opposition/
        noncompliance, **11:**23 (tab)
    tips for school phobia, **11:**21 (tips)
    tips for teachers of, **11:**18 (tab)
    tips for temper tantrums,
        11:25–26
    tips for test-taking, **11:**22 (tab)
    trends/issues influencing,
        11:35–37
Emotional problems, **11:**17, **11:**47
Employment, sheltered/ supported,
    5:25, **5:**56
Empowerment movement, **7:**47

Enhanced image devices,
    7:36–37, 7:60
Enrichment, 3:10, 3:78,
    13:23–24, 13:28–36, 13:53
Enright, B., 3:21
Entwistle, D., 4:5
Entwistle, N., 4:5
Epidural hematomas, 8:26, 8:64
Epilepsy, 8:23, 8:64
Epilepsy Foundation
    of America, 8:47
Epstein, A., 5:16
Epstein, J. L.
Equal access, 2:14, 2:41 (tab), 45–46
Equal protection clause,
    2:7–8, 2:53, 2:55
ERIC Clearinghouse on Disabilities
    and Gifted Education, 1:11
Erin, J. N., 7:8
Error analysis, 3:38, 3:78
Errors
    assessment, 3:62–63
    halo effect, 3:62
    integration, 3:48
    logical, 3:62
    of central tendency, 3:62
    of leniency, 3:62
    perseveration, 3:38, 3:48
    rotation, 3:48
    sensitivity, 3:62
Errors of central tendency, 3:62
Errors of leniency, 3:62
Ethell, R. G., 4:5
Evaluation
    defining, 4:64
    formative, 4:23, 4:64
    language, 10:44
    process, 1:24
    program, 3:16–17, 3:80
    progress, 1:24, 3:80
    protection in procedures,
        1:13, 1:42, 2:21–23, 2:56
    speech, 10:44
    summative, 4:23, 4:65
Event recording, 3:46, 3:78
Exceptional students, defining, 1:41
Exceptionality decisions,
    3:12, 3:78–79

Exclusion, 2:19 (fig),
    2:42 (tab), 2:49–50
Expressive language, 10:43

Face validity, 3:57, 3:79
Families/community agencies. See
    Community collaboration;
    Early intervention; Family
    involvement; Transition
    services
Family involvement, 5:7
    adverse affects of disability on
        family, 5:38
    affect of exceptionalities on
        families, 5:35–37
    gifted student concerns, 5:37–38
    home–school
        collaboration barriers, 5:41
        (tab)–42 (tab)
    home–school collaboration
        barriers, overcoming,
        5:39–40, 5:42
    institutionalization vs. home care
        issues, 5:38
    types of, 5:39
    with communication disorders,
        10:30
FAPE (free and appropriate
    education), 2:55
Fazzi, D. L., 7:7, 7:11
Feedback
    auditory, 7:37
    corrective/supportive, 4:46–47,
        12:37, 12:43
    defining, 4:21, 4:64
    tactile, 7:31
Fetal alcohol syndrome,
    5:10, 8:14, 8:64
Finger spelling, 7:40, 7:60
Flexible promotion, 13:25
Flexible scheduling,
    3:71, 4:54, 4:64
Flexible settings, 3:71, 4:54, 4:64
Fluency disorder, 10:10, 10:43
Forlenza-Bailey, A., 4:5
Formal assessments, 3:11
Formal interviews, 3:30
Formal observations, 3:27, 3:29

Formal tests, **3**:27, **3**:79
Formative evaluation, **4**:23, **4**:64
Forster, G., **6**:53
Foster, R., **10**:27
Foster homes, **5**:31–32
Frederick L. v. Thomas,
    2:39 (tab)–40 (tab)
Free and appropriate education
    (FAPE), **2**:55
Frequency, **7**:20 (tab), **7**:60
Fristoe, M., **10**:26
Fuchs, D., **9**:17
Full inclusion, **6**:21
Functional academic assessment,
    9:19, **9**:57
Functional behavioral assessment,
    9:19, **9**:57, **11**:15–16, **11**:47
Functional hearing losses, **7**:24, **7**:25
    (tab), **7**:60
Funding, **6**:15, **6**:16–17, **6**:44

Gallagher, J., **13**:11,
    13:19, **13**:20, **13**:45
Gallaudet Research Institute
    (GRI), **7**:22
Gallup, A. M., **11**:39
Gardner, H., **13**:43
Giangreco, M. F., **12**:59
Gickling, E., **3**:20
Giddan, J. J., **10**:27
Gifted, defining, **13**:53
Gifted and Talented Children's
    Education Act, **1**:33–34,
    13:10–11
Gifted and talented students
    academic characteristics of,
        13:18–19
    behavioral characteristics of,
        13:20–21
    characteristics of,
        13:15–22, **13**:16 (tab)–17 (tab)
    cognitive characteristics of,
        13:15–18
    communication characteristics of,
        13:21–22
    concerns of families with,
        5:37–38
    creative ability, **1**:34, **1**:40

creative-productive giftedness,
    13:43
criteria other than intelligence
    test to determine, **13**:42–43
defining, **1**:16, **1**:41
evolving concept of giftedness,
    13:41–42
federal legislation concerning,
    13:9–11
identifying gifts/talents, **1**:35–36
identifying students as, **13**:12–14
intellectual ability of, **1**:34
leadership ability of, **1**:35
physical characteristics of,
    13:19–20
schoolhouse
    giftedness, **13**:43
specific academic ability, **1**:34–35
state definitions of, **13**:11–12
terms used to describe,
    13:10 (tab)
underrepresented groups in
    category of, **13**:44–45
visual/performing arts ability of,
    1:35, **1**:40
See also Gifted and talented
    students, teaching
Gifted and talented students,
    teaching
    acceleration tactics, **13**:36–40
    acceleration/advancement
        approach, **13**:25–27
    criteria other than intelligence
        test, **13**:42–43
    enrichment approach, **13**:23–24
    enrichment tactics, **13**:28–36
    extending knowledge in content
        areas, **13**:31–33
    extending knowledge into new
        areas, **13**:33–36 (fig)
    practicing/polishing skills,
        13:28–31 (fig)
    teacher tips, **13**:24 (tab), **13**:45–46
    trends/issues influencing,
        13:41–46
Glaser, W., **4**:43
Goals 2000: The Educate America
    Act, **6**:31, **6**:33

adult literacy/lifelong learning,
    6:27–28
advocacy, **6:**12–13
applying to child with special
    needs, **6:**30
mathematics/science, **6:**27
overview of, **6:**22,
    6:23 (tab)–**6:**24 (tab)
parental participation, **6:**29
safe/disciplined and
    alcohol-/drug-free
    schools, **6:**28–29
school completion, **6:**24–25
school readiness, **6:**22, **6:**24
standards, **6:**31, **6:**33
student achievement/
    citizenship, **6:**25–26
teacher education/ professional
    development, **6:**26–27
See also Individuals With
    Disabilities Education Act;
    No Child Left Behind Act
Goldman, R., **10:**26
Good, T., **4:**13
Goss v. Lopez, **2:**39 (tab)
Grammar, **10:**44
Grand mal (tonic-clonic) seizures,
    8:23, **8:**64
Gray Oral Reading Test–4, **3:**37
Greene, J. P., **6:**53
Greenwood, C., **3:**22, **4:**46
Greer, B. B., **8:**49
Greer, J. G., **8:**49
GRI (Gallaudet Research
    Institute), **7:**22
Griffin, N. S., **13:**11
Grossman, H., **12:**24–25
Group data, **3:**50
Group homes, **5:**30–31, **5:**55
Group-administered
    tests, **3:**27, **3:**79
Gruenewald, L., **12:**67
Guertin, T. L., **13:**45
Guide dogs, **4:**55

Hairston v. Drosick, **2:**39 (tab)
Hall, V., **4:**46
Halo effect errors, **3:**62

Haloed, **3:**56
Handicapped Children's
    Early Education
    Assistance Act, **5:**11
Handicapped Children's Protection
    Act, **2:**48–49, **2:**55
Harcourt Educational
    Measurement, **3:**37
Hard-of-hearing
    defining, **7:**18–19, **7:**21, **7:**60
    See also Hearing impairments
Hart, C. A., **8:**30
Haskins, R., **5:**15
Havertape, J., **3:**20
Head Start, **5:**11, **5:**15,
    5:55, **6:**7, **6:**9
HeadSmart Schools program,
    8:27–28
Hearing acuity, **3:**40
Hearing aid, **4:**50–51, **4:**64, **7:**41
    troubleshooting, **7:**50–51
Hearing impairments
    academic characteristics of,
        7:23–24
    behavioral characteristics of,
        7:24–27
    central hearing losses, **7:**57
    cognitive characteristics of,
        7:22–23
    communication characteristics of,
        7:27–28 (tab)
    conductive hearing losses,
        7:19, **7:**56
    deaf culture and, **7:**26, **7:**59
    defining, **7:**6, **7:**18, **7:**60
    educational implications of,
        7:57–58
    ethnicity and, **7:**26
    functional hearing losses, **7:**24,
        7:25 (tab), **7:**60
    history of schools for deaf
        students, **7:**17–18
    integrating deaf/hearing
        students, **7:**26–27
    manual communication
        for, **7:**58
    measuring hearing loss, **7:**19–21
    mixed hearing losses, **7:**57

oral communication for, **7:**58
prevalence of, **7:**21–22, **7:**56
senorineural losses, **7:**19, **7:**56–57
signs of, **7:**28 (tab)
teacher tips, **7:**28 (tab)
technology for, **7:**58
total communication for, **7:**58
See also Deaf-and-blind/
deaf-blind
Heart conditions, **8:**12, **8:**64
Hebbeler, K., **5:**24
Hematomas, **8:**26, **8:**64
subdural, **8:**26, **8:**66
Hemophilia, **8:**13, **8:**59, **8:**64
Henderson, A. T., **5:**42 (tab)
*Hendrick Hudson District Board
of Education v. Rowley,*
2:41 (tab), **2:**45–46
Highly qualified teacher, **2:**31–32
Ho, A. S. P., **4:**5
Hobson v. Hansen, **2:**36 (tab)
Hodgkinson, H. L., 44
Holmes, D. L., **8:**29
Home-based programs,
5:12–14, **5:**55
Homeless child/wards of
court, **2:**34
Homework buddies, **9:**38–39
Honig v. Doe, **2:**19 (fig), **2:**42 (tab),
2:49–50
Hospital-based programs, **5:**13–14,
5:55
Humphries, T., **7:**26
Hunsaker, S. L., **1:**35–36
Hyperactivity-impulsivity, **9:**23–24,
9:45 (tab), **9:**57
Hyperopia, **7:**9–10, **7:**60

IDEA. *See* Individuals With
Disabilities Education Act
IDEIA. *See* Individuals With
Disabilities Education
Improvement Act
IEP. *See* Individualized education
programs
IFSP (individualized family service
plan), **2:**25, **2:**54, **2:**55, **12:**71
Imber-Black, E., **5:**42 (tab)

Immaturity, **3:**47
Immunodeficiency, **8:**12
Inattention, **9:**46–47, **9:**57
Incidental learning, **7:**14
In-class field trip, for math skills,
12:42 (fig)
Inclusion, **1:**21–22, **1:**41, **6:**21, **6:**38–39
as school reform, **6:**21, **6:**38–39
defining, **6:**45
full, **6:**21
mainstreaming as, **2:**54, **2:**56,
5:29–30, **5:**56
of student with medical/
physical/multiple
disabilities, **8:**56–59,
8:57 (tab)
of student with mental
retardation, **12:**67–68
technology role in, **6:**38–39
See also Least restrictive
environment
Independent living,
5:23, **5:**30, **5:**32, **8:**31,
12:31, **12:**55, **12:**58
Independent practice, **4:**40, **10:**36–37
Indirect (consultative)
services, **1:**26, **1:**40,
1:41, **5:**12, **5:**55
Individual data, **3:**50
Individual family service plan
(IFSP), **5:**12, **5:**55, **12:**33
Individualized education programs
(IEP), **1:**13, **1:**23–24, **2:**54, **8:**43
amendments to, **2:**33
decision-making process
and, **2:**23–2:24
defining, **1:**42, **2:**55, **3:**79
due process hearing, **2:**21
for student with communication
disorder, **10:**41–42
for student with mental
retardation, **12:**6–7,
12:33, **12:**71
individualized family
service plan, **2:**25,
2:54, **2:**55, **12:**71
least restrictive environment
requirement of, **2:**23

measurable goals requirement of,
    2:17, 2:28
prior written notice requirement
    of, 2:21
protection in evaluation
    procedures provision
    of, 2:21
reasons for, 2:17, 2:20
sample of, 2:18 (fig)–19 (fig)
team members required by,
    2:20 (fig)
Individualized family service plan
    (IFSP), 2:25, 2:54, 2:55, 12:71
Individualized transition plan (ITP),
    2:26, 2:55–56, 5:23,
    5:56, 12:63, 12:71
Individually administered tests, 3:27
Individuals With Disabilities
    Education Act (IDEA),
    2:12 (tab), 2:25–26, 2:54
assistive technologies under, 2:26
defining, 2:56
discrimination protection, 1:13
mandates of, 1:12–13,
    4:54, 6:37–38
on educational settings, 1:31–32
on emotional disturbance, 11:7–8,
    11:35–36
on learning disabilities, 9:7–8, 9:9
on mental retardation, 12:9
on transition services, 5:23
preschool services under,
    5:10–11 (fig)
See also Education for All
    Handicapped Children Act;
    Individuals With Disabilities
    Education Act (IDEA),
    amendments to; Individuals
    With Disabilities Education
    Improvement Act; Least
    restrictive environment
Individuals With Disabilities
    Education Act (IDEA),
    amendments to
discipline policies, 2:28–29
individualized education
    program, 2:28
manifestation determination, 2:29

parental consent for reevaluation,
    2:12 (tab), 2:27
preschoolers, 5:12
streamlined reevaluation, 2:27–28
Individuals With Disabilities
    Education Improvement Act
    (IDEIA), 2:13, 2:25–26, 2:56
assessment language/
    communication mode,
    2:32–33
highly qualified teacher
    requirement, 2:31–32
homeless child/wards
    of court, 2:34
individualized education
    program provisions, 2:33
learning disabled
    identification, 2:32
special education students in
    general education, 2:33
transition planning, 2:33
Inference, 3:61–62, 3:79
Informal interviews, 3:30, 3:79
Informal observations,
    3:27, 3:29, 3:44
Informal tests, 3:27, 3:79
Institutions, for adults with
    special needs, 5:33
Instruction
computer-assisted, 4:5
defining, 4:5, 4:7, 4:64
teaching as, 4:5
See also Direct instruction,
    principles of; Instruction,
    adapting for students with
    special needs; Instruction,
    delivering; Instruction,
    evaluating; Instruction,
    managing; Instruction,
    planning
Instruction, adapting for students
    with special
    needs, 4:31–38
ability training, 4:39–40
behavior therapy, 4:38
classwide peer tutoring, 4:47
cognitive behavior modification,
    4:41, 4:42 (fig)

cognitive skills training, **4**:41, **4**:43
cooperative learning, **4**:45–46
counseling therapy, **4**:43–45
critical thinking, **4**:43
direct instruction, **4**:40
learning strategies training, **4**:45
peer tutoring, **4**:46
peer-directed learning, **4**:46
precision teaching, **4**:39
social skills training, **4**:47–48
Instruction, delivering, **4**:17–23
adjusting instruction, **4**:21 (tab),
    4:22–23
monitoring student learning,
    4:21 (tab)–22
motivating students, **4**:20
overview of, **4**:18 (tab)
presenting content, **4**:17–20
presenting lessons, **4**:17–19
providing relevant
    practice, **4**:20
teaching thinking skills, **4**:19–20
Instruction, evaluating, **4**:23–29
informing students of
    progress, **4**:27
maintaining student progress
    records, **4**:26 (fig)–27
making judgments about student
    performance, **4**:28 (fig)–29
monitoring engaged time, **4**:25
monitoring student
    understanding, **4**:23–25
overview of, **4**:24 (tab)
using data to make decisions,
    4:27–28
Instruction, managing, **4**:14–17
creating positive environment,
    4:16–17
overview of, **4**:15 (tab)
preparing for instruction,
    4:15–16
using time productively, **4**:16
Instruction, planning, **4**:7–14
actively involving
    students, **4**:14
analyzing groupings, **4**:10–11
analyzing task, **4**:10
assessing student skills, **4**:9

communicating realistic
    expectations, **4**:13–14
considering contextual
    variables, **4**:10
deciding how to teach, **4**:11–13
deciding what to teach, **4**:9–11
establishing gaps in actual/
    expected performance, **4**:11
establishing sequence, **4**:10
explicitly stating
    expectations, **4**:14
maintaining high
    standards, **4**:14
monitoring
    performance/replanning
    instruction, **4**:13
overview of, **4**:8 (tab)
pacing, **4**:13
selecting methods/materials,
    4:12–13
setting goals, **4**:12
Instructional adaptations, to
    increase communication/
    motility, **4**:49–50
amplification systems, **4**:51
braille, **4**:52, **7**:10, **7**:13,
    7:15, **7**:16, **7**:34, **7**:35 (tab)
calculators, **4**:53
canes, **4**:55
communication
    boards, **4**:50
computers, **4**:53–54
electronic travel aids, **4**:55–56
guide dogs, **4**:55
hearing aids, **4**:50–51
Kurzweil reading
    machines, **4**:53
optacons, **4**:52–53
prostheses, **4**:56–57
telecommunication devices,
    4:51–52
test modifications, **4**:54
wheelchairs, **4**:56
Instructional diagnosis, **3**:22, **3**:79
Instructional programs, keys
    to success in, **5**:47–50
commitment to normal life
    experiences, **5**:49

commitment to remedial
 programming, **5**:49
compatible physical
 environment, **5**:49
encouraging appropriate
 behavior, **5**:50
individualized planning, **5**:48–49
lifelong learning, **5**:50
Integration errors, **3**:48
Intellectual abilities, **1**:34, **1**:42, **2**:32,
 3:34–37, **9**:9
 intelligence interviews, **3**:36–37
 observing intelligence, **3**:34, 36
 overview of, **3**:35 (tab)–36 (tab)
 testing intelligence, **3**:34
Intellectual functioning, **12**:71
Intelligence. *See* Intellectual abilities
International Baccalaureate
 (IB), **13**:26
Interval recording, **3**:45, **3**:79
Intervention assistance. *See*
 Prereferral interventions
Intervention assistance team (IAT),
 3:10, **3**:79
Interviews, **3**:26, **3**:30–31
 academic achievement,
 assessing, **3**:38–39
 formal, **3**:30
 informal, **3**:30, **3**:79
 intelligence, **3**:36–37
 language, **3**:44
 perceptual-motor, **3**:48
 psychological, **3**:46–47
 structured, **3**:30
 to assess academic achievement,
 3:38–39
 unstructured, **3**:30
Irrelevant activity, **11**:31, **11**:47
*Irving Independent School District v.
 Tatro*, **2**:42 (tab), **2**:46, **2**:54
ITP (individualized transition plan),
 2:26, **2**:55–56, **5**:23, **5**:56,
 12:63, **12**:71

Jackson, D. W., **7**:23, **7**:24,
 7:27, **7**:40, **7**:42
Jakob K. Javits Gifted and Talented
 Students Act, **13**:11

Jatho, J., **7**:26, **7**:42
Job coach, **5**:25, **5**:48, **5**:56, **12**:54
Johnson, D. W., **4**:45
Johnson, F., **12**:67
Johnson, N. E., **13**:45
Johnson, R. T., **4**:45
Jorgensen, J., **12**:67
Journals/articles (resources)
 assessment, **3**:92–93
 communication disorders,
 10:57–58
 emotional disturbance, **11**:60–63
 fundamentals of special
 education, **1**:54–55
 gifted and talented child, **13**:64
 learning disabilities, **9**:67–68
 legal foundations, **2**:66
 medical/physical/multiple
 disabilities, **8**:80–82
 mental retardation, **12**:84–85
 public policy/school
 reform, **6**:56
 sensory disabilities, **7**:77–79
 transitions, **5**:67
Juvenile rheumatoid arthritis,
 8:20, **8**:64

Kanner, Leo, **8**:29
Kember, D., **4**:5
Kentucky School System
 reform, **6**:34–35
*Kevin T. v. Elmhurst Community
 School District No.*, **2**:44 (tab)
Key Points
 assessment, **3**:75–76
 communication disorders,
 10:42–43
 effective instruction, **4**:61–62
 emotional disturbance, **11**:43–46
 fundamentals, **1**:39–40
 gifted and talented child,
 13:51–52
 learning disabilities, **9**:55–56
 legal foundations, **2**:53–54
 medical/physical/multiple
 disabilities, **8**:61–62
 mental retardation,
 12:69–70

public policy/school reform,
  6:43–44
sensory disabilities, **7**:53–58
transitions, **5**:53–54
Key Vocabulary
  assessment, **3**:76–81
  communication disorders,
    10:43–45
  effective instruction, **4**:62–66
  emotional disturbance, **11**:46–47
  families/community agencies,
    5:54–56
  fundamentals, **1**:40–43
  gifted and talented child,
    13:52–53
  learning disabilities, **9**:56–57
  legal foundations, **2**:54–56
  medical/physical/multiple
    disabilities, **8**:62–66
  mental retardation, **12**:70–72
  public policy/school reform,
    6:44–46
  sensory disabilities, **7**:59–62
Kirk, S. A., **9**:51
Klinefelter syndrome, **12**:14, **12**:71
Koestler, F., **7**:8
Koppitz, E. M., **3**:47
Kreimeyer, K. H., **7**:26
Kurzweil reading machines, **4**:53
Kwan, K. P., **4**:5

Lagomarcino, T., **5**:24
Lahey, B. B., **9**:44
Language development, **3**:43–44
  language test components, **3**:43
  using interviews, **3**:44
  using observations, **3**:44
Language disorders, **10**:44
Language evaluation, **10**:44
Larry P v. Riles, **2**:38 (tab)–39 (tab),
  6:10, **6**:45
Larsen, L. M., **13**:11
Larsen, M. D., **13**:11
Latency recording, **3**:46, **3**:80
Law, continuing changes in, **2**:7
Lead poisoning, **8**:11 (tab), **8**:64
Leadership ability, **1**:35, **1**:42,
  13:10, **13**:42

Learning centers,
  for reading, **9**:31
Learning disabilities (LDs)
  academic, **9**:51
  academic characteristics
    of, **9**:23
  assessing, **9**:17–19
  behavioral characteristics of,
    9:23–24
  category growth, **9**:12, **9**:14
  causes of, **9**:15–16
  cognitive characteristics of, **9**:22
  communication characteristics of,
    9:24–25
  criteria for identifying, **9**:8–9
  defining, **9**:7–8, **9**:49–50, **9**:57
  defining, variations by state,
    9:51–52
  developmental, **9**:51
  discrepancy criterion
    removal, **9**:9
  distribution of students
    with, by state, **9**:13
    (tab)–**9**:14 (tab)
  growth in specific learning
    disabilities category, **9**:11–12
  physical characteristics
    of, **9**:23
  prevalence of, **9**:11
  subtypes of, **9**:51
  transition of students
    with, **9**:52
  See also Learning disabilities
    (LDs), improving classroom
    behavior for students with;
    Learning disabilities (LDs),
    teaching students with
Learning disabilities (LDs),
    improving classroom behavior
    for students with
  daily reports, **9**:37 (fig)
  homework buddies,
    9:38–39
  study skills, **9**:37–39
  work habits, **9**:35–37
Learning disabilities (LDs),
    teaching students with,
    9:25–41

general interventions, **9:**26 (tab)
math skills, **9:**32–33
reading skills, **9:**27–32
social relations, **9:**39–41
study skills, **9:**37–39
trends/issues influencing
    teaching of, **9:**49–52
work habits, **9:**35–37
written language skills, **9:**33–35
Learning strategies training,
    4:45, **4:**64
Least restrictive environment (LRE),
    1:13, **1:**27–28, **2:**23, **2:**41, **2:**54,
    2:56, **12:**61
    defining, **5:**30, **5:**56, **12:**71
Ledesma, J., **4:**5
Lee, V. E., **5:**15
Leff, D., **7:**11, **7:**15
Legal fees, **2:**42 (tab), **2:**46–48
Legal foundations, of special
    education
    balance perspective in, **2:**51–52
    brief history of, **2:**9–10
    early issues in, **2:**44–45
    overview of important laws,
        2:10–11
    overview of influential court
        cases, **2:**36 (tab)–44 (tab)
    Supreme Court rulings, **2:**45–50
    See also *individual laws and
        individual cases*
Legally blind, **7:**9, **7:**60
Legg-Calvé-Perthes disease,
    8:21, **8:**64
Lehr, C., **5:**18
Lehr, F., **9:**28
Lemon v. Bossier Parish School Board,
    2:38 (tab)
Leukemia, **8:**11 (tab), **8:**64
Leventhal, J. D., **7:**36
Levine, D. U., **4:**5–6
Levy, S. E., **8:**15
Lewis, R. B., **8:**56–58, **8:**57 (tab),
    10:18–20
Lieberman, L., **7:**29
Lifelong learning, **5:**50, **6:**27–28
Light v. Parkway School District,
    2:43 (tab)

Liles, C., **8:**15–16, **8:**43, **8:**55–56
Limb deficiencies, **8:**21–22, **8:**64
Listening-skills training,
    7:34, **7:**35 (tab)
Living arrangements, for adults
    with special needs
    alternative living unit, **5:**31
    foster homes, **5:**31–32
    group homes, **5:**30–31
    independent living, **5:**32
    institutions, **5:**33
Lloyd, J., **4:**40
Logical errors, **3:**62
Long, E., **12:**67
*Lora v. New York City Board of
    Education,* **2:**40 (tab)–41 (tab)
Loudness, **7:**19–20, **7:**60
Louisiana Department of Education,
    13:12
Low vision, **7:**60–61
Luckner, J., **7:**24, **7:**38, **7:**42, **7:**50
Luetke-Stahlman, B., **7:**24, **7:**42, **7:**50
Lynch, E. W., **8:**56–58, **8:**57 (tab)

Mainstreaming, **2:**54, **2:**56,
    5:29–30, **5:**56
    See also Least restrictive
        environment
Mangrum, C. II, **5:**26
Manifestation determination,
    2:29, **2:**56
Manual movements, **7:**40, **7:**61
Marburger, C. L., **5:**42 (tab)
Marder, C., **5:**24
Marland, S., **13:**41–42
Maryland State Department of
    Education, **13:**11
Mastery, defining, **9:**32
Mathematics, improving,
    6:27, **9:**32–33, **9:**34 (fig)
McBurnett, K., **9:**44
McKinney, J. D., **9:**51
McMeniman, M. M., **4:**5
Measures of process disorders,
    9:18–19
Medical disabilities, **8:**9–16
    AIDS, **8:**12–13
    cystic fibrosis, **8:**12

fetal alcohol syndrome, **8:**14
heart conditions, **8:**12
hemophilia, **8:**13–14
identification by medical
    symptoms, **8:**9–10
maternal cocaine use, **8:**14–15
medically fragile/technology
    dependent groups, **8:**15–16
other health impairments,
    8:10–11 (tab)
prevalence of, **8:**10
special health problems, **8:**14–15
Medical procedures, to ensure
    appropriate education,
    2:46, **2:**48, **2:**54
Medical treatment, for emotional
    disturbance, **11:**37–38
Medically fragile, **8:**15, **8:**64
Medical/physical/multiple
    disabilities
    academic characteristics
        of, **8:**38
    behavioral characteristics of,
        8:39–40
    cognitive characteristics of,
        8:37–38
    communication characteristics of,
        8:40–41
    distribution of child with, **8:**7–8
        (fig)
    home *vs.* institutional care for,
        8:55–56
    inclusion of student with, **8:**56
    inclusion of student with,
        overcoming barriers to,
        8:56–59, **8:**57 (tab)
    medical disabilities, **8:**9–16,
        8:10–11 (tab)
    multiple disabilities, **8:**33–35
    physical characteristics of, **8:**39
    physical disabilities,
        8:17–31, **8:**25 (tab)
    relationship to federal disability
        categories, **8:**7 (fig)
    See also Medical/
        physical/multiple
        disabilities, teaching
        students with

Medical/physical/multiple
    disabilities, teaching students
    with, **8:**43–53
    adapting instruction, **8:**47–49
    common adaptations, **8:**49–50
    encouraging socialization, **8:**53
    facilitating communication,
        8:50–52
    fostering independence, **8:**52–53
    general tips for, **8:**45 (tab)
    identifying disabilities, **8:**44
    key areas of assistance, **8:**46–47
    questions to ask about, **8:**44, **8:**45
        (tab)–**8:**46 (tab)
    residual functioning, **8:**52–53
Mental retardation, **1:**16, **1:**42
    academic characteristics of, **12:**30
    as primary/secondary condition,
        12:28
    behavioral characteristics
        of, **12:**31
    characteristics of, **12:**2 (tab)
    cognitive characteristics
        of, **12:**30
    communication characteristics of,
        12:31–32
    defining, **12:**6, **12:**9, **12:**71
    genetic conditions as cause
        of, **12:**13–14
    graduation rates of student with,
        12:63–64
    health problems as cause
        of, **12:**15
    inclusion of student with,
        12:67–68
    individualized education
        program, **12:**6–7
    learning environments for
        student with, **12:**67
    mild/moderate/severe/
        profound retardation, **12:**10
        (fig)–**12:**11 (tab)
    physical characteristics of,
        12:30–31
    prevalence of, **12:**11
    preventing, **12:**62 (tab)
    problems during pregnancy/
        birth as cause of, **12:**15

recent advances in treatment/
services, **12**:65–67
self-determination
and, **12**:64
transitioning from school to
work, **12**:63–64
See also Mental retardation,
diagnosing; Mental
retardation, teaching
students with
Mental retardation, diagnosing,
12:17–25
adaptive behavior area,
12:17, **12**:19–25
adaptive behavior, defining,
12:21
adaptive behavior scales, **12**:21
adaptive skill areas evaluated,
12:21 (tab)–23 (tab)
age-related criteria for, **12**:24–25
intellectual functioning
area, **12**:17
Mental retardation, teaching
students with, **12**:33–51
by making adaptations, **12**:33–34
family tips for, **12**:34,
12:36 (tab)
functional math skills,
12:41–42 (fig)
functional reading skills, **12**:38–41
(fig), **12**:39 (fig), **12**:40
(fig), **12**:41 (fig), 40 (fig)
functional writing, **12**:40
general interventions for,
12:37 (tab)
grading systems for, **12**:47–49
individualized education
program, **12**:33
individualized family services
plan, **12**:33
leisure skills, **12**:50–51
school adaptive behavior,
12:45–49
task analysis, **12**:43–45
task completion, **12**:38
teacher tips for, **12**:35 (tab)
trends/issues influencing,
12:61–64

work skills, **12**:49–50
See also Severe disabilities,
teaching student with
Metropolitan Achievement Tests, **3**:37
Meyer, C., **3**:39
Meyer, L. H., **12**:55
Michaud, L. J., **8**:25, **8**:26, **8**:27
Mild/moderate/severe/
profound retardation,
12:10 (fig)–**12**:11 (tab)
Miller, L., **3**:21
Minitests, **9**:30 (fig), **9**:57
*Minnesota Standards for
Services to Gifted and
Talented Students*, **13**:12
Minnesota State Advisory
Council for the Gifted
and Talented, **13**:12
Mizuko, M., **10**:16
Mobility, **7**:14, **7**:61
Mobility aids, **7**:34, **7**:35 (tab)
Mock, D., **9**:17
Molloy, D. E., **9**:17–18
Moore, S. D., **1**:35–36
Moores, D., **7**:17, **7**:21,
7:23, **7**:24–25, **7**:26, **7**:42
Moran, M., **6**:41
Morgan, P. L., **9**:17
Morphology, **10**:10–11, **10**:44
Mowat Sensor, **4**:55–56
Muir, S., **7**:38
Multiple disabilities, **8**:34–35
Multiple intelligences, **13**:43, **13**:53
Multiple or severe
disabilities, **1**:16, **1**:42
See also Severe disabilities,
teaching student with
Multiple sclerosis, **8**:20–21
Murphy, D. S., **8**:56–58, **8**:57 (tab)
Muscular dystrophy, **8**:19–20, **8**:65
Myelomeningocele, **8**:24
Myopia, **7**:9, **7**:61

NAGC (National Association for
Gifted Children), **13**:25–27
Nania, P. A., **5**:18
*A Nation at Risk: The Imperative for
Educational Reform*, **6**:19–20

National Association for
    Gifted Children (NAGC),
    13:25–27
National Association
    of the Deaf, **7**:42
National Autistic Society, **8**:28
National Center for Education
    Statistics, **1**:31, **5**:9, **5**:10
National Commission on Excellence
    in Education, **6**:19–20
National Council on Educational
    Standards and Testing, **6**:31–32
National Dissemination Center for
    Children with Disabilities
    (NICHY), **11**:44–46
National Education Goals,
    5:10, **6**:19–20, **6**:45
National Educational
    Standards and Improvement
    Council, **6**:31
National Governors' Association,
    6:20, **6**:34
National Head Injury Foundation
    (NHIF), **8**:27–28
National Information Center, **10**:38
National Institute on Deafness and
    Other Communication
    Disorders Information
    Clearinghouse, **7**:58
National Joint Committee on
    Learning Disabilities (NJCLD),
    9:15, **9**:50
National Research Council, **1**:13
Nechita, A., **1**:35
Needs assessments, **4**:41, **4**:64
Nephrosis/nephritis,
    8:11 (tab), **8**:65
Neurological disorders, **8**:22–25
    cerebral palsy, **8**:23–24
    epilepsy, **8**:23
    overview of, **8**:25 (tab)
    spina bifida, **8**:24
    spinal cord injury, **8**:24–25
Newland, T. E.,
    7:12–13, **7**:30
Newman, L., **5**:24
NHIF (National Head Injury
    Foundation), **8**:27–28

NICHY (National Dissemination
    Center for Children with
    Disabilities), **11**:44–46
NJCLD (National Joint Committee
    on Learning Disabilities),
    9:15, **9**:50
No Child Left Behind Act, **2**:12 (tab),
    2:29–31, **2**:54, **6**:10, **6**:37–38, **6**:45
Nonattention (distractibility),
    11:29–30, **11**:47
Noncategorical, **12**:18, **12**:71
Noncompliance (oppositional
    behavior), **11**:22–24, **11**:47
Nonmanual movements, **7**:40, **7**:61
Nonphysical disruptions,
    11:27–28, **11**:47
Normal field of vision, **7**:9, **7**:61
Normalization, **12**:61, **12**:72
Normative peer comparisons,
    4:28, **4**:64
Norm-referenced tests,
    3:29, **3**:80, **4**:9, **4**:64
Norms, **3**:8–9, **3**:80
Nystagmus, **7**:10, **7**:61

Objective-referenced test. *See*
    Criterion-referenced tests
Observations, **3**:25–26, **3**:29–30
    active, **3**:29, **3**:77
    defining, **3**:80
    formal, **3**:29
    informal, **3**:27, **3**:29, **3**:44
    language, **3**:44
    of achievement, **3**:38
    of sensory acuity, **3**:40–41
    passive, **3**:29, **3**:80
    perceptual-motor, **3**:48
Occupational and
    social skills, **3**:42
OCR (Optical character recognition),
    7:36 (tab),
    7:38, **7**:61
Ocular motility, **7**:10, **7**:61
Oden, M., **13**:20, **13**:41, **13**:42
Office of Civil Rights, **6**:11, **6**:13
Office of Educational Research
    and Improvement, **13**:45,
    13:48, **13**:49

Office of Special
    Education Programs (OSEP),
    6:13–14, **6:**45
Ogbu, J. U., **13:**48
On Your Own
    assessment, **3:**89
    communication
        disorders, **10:**55
    effective instruction, **4:**73
    emotional disturbance, **11:**55–56
    families/community
        agencies, **5:**63
    fundamentals of special
        education, **1:**51
    gifted and talented child,
        13:61–62
    learning disabilities, **9:**65–66
    legal foundations of special
        education, **2:**63
    medical/physical/multiple
        disabilities, **8:**73–74
    mental retardation, **12:**79
    public policy/school
        reform, **6:**53
    sensory disabilities, **7:**69–71
Ooms, T., **5:**42 (tab)
Operant conditioning,
    4:38, **4:**65
Opportunity-to-learn (OTL)
    standards, **4:**46, **6:**12,
    6:33, **6:**45
Oppositional behavior
    (noncompliance),
    11:22–24, **11:**47
Optacons, **4:**52–53
Optical character recognition (OCR),
    7:36 (tab), **7:**38, **7:**61
Oral communication,
    for students with
    vision/hearing impairments,
    7:39–40, **7:**39 (tab)
Organizations (resources)
    assessment, **3:**93
    communication disorders,
        10:58–59
    effective instruction, **4:**77
    emotional disturbance,
        11:63–65

fundamentals of special
    education, **1:**54–55
gifted and talented child, **13:**65
learning disabilities, **9:**68–69
medical/physical/multiple
    disabilities, **8:**83–84
mental retardation, **12:**86–87
public policy/school reform,
    6:56–57
sensory disabilities, **7:**79–85
transitions, **5:**68
Orientation, **7:**14, **7:**61
Ornstein, A. C., **4:**5–6
Orr, A. L., **7:**7, **7:**11, **7:**13,
    7:14, **7:**15, **7:**34
Orr, S., **4:**5
Orthopedic impairments,
    8:17–18, **8:**65
    prevalence of, **8:**18
Orthopedic or other health
    impairments, **1:**16–17, **1:**42
Orthosis, **8:**52, **8:**65
Osborn, J., **9:**28
OSEP (Office of Special Education
    Programs), **6:**13–14, **6:**45
Osteogenesis imperfecta, **8:**20, **8:**65
Osteomyelitis, **8:**21, **8:**65
O'Sullivan, P. J., **5:**18
OTL (Opportunity-to-learn)
    standards, **4:**46, **6:**12, **6:**33, **6:**45
Outcomes-based
    accountability, **3:**23, **6:**35

Pace, **4:**13, **4:**65
Panitch v. State of Wisconsin,
    2:40 (tab)
Parental participation, **6:**29
Partially sighted, **7:**61
PASE v. Hannon, **2:**41 (tab)
Passive observation, **3:**29
Pathsounder, **4:**55
Paul, P. V., **7:**23, **7:**24,
    7:27, **7:**40, **7:**42
Paulson, F., **3:**39
Paulson, P., **3:**39
Peavey, K. O., **7:**11, **7:**15
Peck, C. A., **12:**55
Peer tutoring, **4:**46–47, **4:**65

Peer tutoring, classwide,
    4:47, **4:**63
Peer-directed learning, **4:**46
*Pennsylvania Association of Retarded
    Citizens v. Commonwealth of
    Pennsylvania,* **12:**65–66
PEP (protection in evaluation
    procedures), **1:**13, **1:**42,
    2:21–23, **2:**56
Perceptual-motor development,
    3:47–48
Perceptual-motor interviews, **3:**48
Perceptual-motor observations, **3:**48
Perceptual-motor tests, **3:**47–48, **3:**80
Performance assessment,
    3:24, **3:**80
Perret, Y. M., **8:**22, **8:**47
Perseveration errors, **3:**38, **3:**48
Perspective
    assessment, **3:**73–74
    communication disorders,
        10:35–38
    effective instruction, **4:**59–60
    emotional disturbance, **11:**39–41
    fundamentals, **1:**37–38
    gifted and talented, **13:**47–49
    learning disabilities, **9:**53–54
    legal foundations, **2:**51–52
    medical/physical/multiple
        disabilities, **8:**55–59
    mental retardation, **12:**65–68
    public policy/school reform,
        6:37–42
    sensory disabilities, **7:**47–51
    transitions, **5:**51–52
Petit mal seizures, **8:**23, **8:**65
Pfiffner, L. J., **9:**44
Phenylketonuria (PKU),
    12:14, **12:**72
Phonetic cues, **9:**29, **9:**57
Phonology, **10:**10–11, **10:**44
Physical disabilities, **8:**17–31
    autism, **8:**28–31
    craniofacial anomalies, **8:**22
    defining, **8:**65
    juvenile rheumatoid
        arthritis, **8:**20
    Legg-Calvé-Perthes disease, **8:**21

limb deficiencies, **8:**21–22
multiple sclerosis, **8:**20–21
muscular dystrophy, **8:**19–20
neurological disorders, **8:**22–25
orthopedic impairments, **8:**17–18
osteogenesis imperfecta, **8:**20
poliomyelitis, **8:**18–19
traumatic brain injury, **1:**17, **1:**43,
    8:25–28, **8:**66
Physical disruptions, **11:**27, **11:**47
Pilmer, S. L., **8:**15
Pogrund, R. L., **7:**7, **7:**11
Poliomyelitis, **8:**18–19, **8:**65
Portfolios, **3:**26, **3:**39, **3:**80
Post-school interventions, **5:**50, **5:**56
Post-school transitions,
    5:23, **5:**24–25, **5:**37
Poteet, J., **3:**21
Powers, M. D., **8:**29, **8:**30
Pragmatics, **10:**11, **10:**44
Pratt, S., **8:**30
Precision teaching, **4:**39, **4:**65
Prereferral interventions
    defining, **1:**9, **1:**22, **1:**42, **3:**80
    determining eligibility, **1:**22
    evolution of, **1:**11–12
    growth in population receiving,
        1:19–20
    individualized education
        programs
        (*See* Individualized
        education programs)
    perspective on, **1:**37–38
    process evaluation, **1:**24
    purpose of, **3:**11
Preschool
    attendance increase, **5:**9–10
    early intervention during, **5:**9–10
    Individuals With Disabilities
        Education Act and, **5:**10–12,
        5:11 (fig)
    transition to K-12 education
        system, **5:**18–19
    Ypsilanti Perry Preschool Project,
        5:15–16
President's Commission on
    Excellence in Special
    Education, **1:**13

Private school, **2:**42 (tab),
    2:46–47, **2:**54
Process disorders, **9:**19, **9:**57
Program evaluation
    defining, **3:**80
    large-scale, **3:**16–17
    teacher's own, **3:**17
Programmed learning,
    13:37, **13:**39, **13:**53
Progress evaluation, **1:**24, **3:**80
Prostheses/prosthetic devices,
    4:56–57, **4:**65, **8:**65
Protection in evaluation procedures
    (PEP), **1:**13, **1:**42, **2:**21–23, **2:**56
Psychoeducational
    assessment, **3:**9, **3:**81
Psychological development,
    assessing, **3:**45–47
    personality tests, **3:**45
    psychological interviews, **3:**46–47
    psychological observations,
        3:45–46
Psychological interviews, **3:**46–47
Public Law 94–142. *See*
    Education for All
    Handicapped Children Act
Public policy
    impact on special education,
        6:39–40
    political effects on, **6:**10–11
    See also School reform
Pupil unit allocation method,
    6:16–17
Purcell, J. H., **13:**45

Quay, H., **3:**46

Rakes, T., **3:**21
Randomization without
    replacement, **4:**60
RAP mnemonic, **4:**45
Rapport, establishing, 60
Reading, improving
    analytical programs for,
        9:27, **9:**56
    fostering motivation/interest,
        9:30–32
    reading comprehension, **9:**28–30

sight word recognition, **9:**28
taped texts for, **9:**6
whole language programs for,
    9:27, **9:**57
Reading Excellence Act, **6:**20
Reading First, **2:**30–31, **6:**10, **6:**20
Reality therapy, **4:**43, **4:**65
Reber, M., **8:**30
Receptive language, **10:**44
Redl, F., **4:**44
Referral, **1:**22, **1:**42
    See also Prereferral interventions
Reflection
    assessment, **3:**3–4, **3:**85–87
    communication disorders,
        10:5, **10:**51
    effective instruction, **4:**4, **4:**70
    emotional disturbance, **11:**3–4,
        11:51–52
    families/community agencies,
        5:3–4, **5:**59–60
    fundamentals of special
        education, **1:**4, **1:**48
    gifted and talented
        child, **13:**3–4, **13:**57–58
    learning disabilities,
        9:3–4, **9:**62
    legal foundations of special
        education, **2:**4, **2:**60
    medical/physical/multiple
        disabilities, **8:**3, **8:**69–70
    mental retardation, **12:**3–4,
        12:75–76
    public policy/school
        reform, **6:**3, **6:**49
    sensory disabilities, **7:**3, **7:**65
Regular education initiative (REI),
    6:21, **6:**45
Rehabilitation Act, **2:**53, **9:**44
Reichert, E. S., **13:**45
Reis, S. M., **13:**45
Related services, **1:**26, **5:**12, **10:**42
    as part of individualized
        education program,
        1:23, **11:**45, **12:**33
    defining, **1:**42–43, **6:**45
    growth in numbers receiving,
        1:19–20

mandated, **1:**31, **2:**48, **6:**40, **8:**17,
    8:43, **12:**9
Related services personnel,
    1:20, **3:**12
Reliability, **3:**50, **3:**81
Reliability coefficient,
    3:50, **3:**81
Remedial education, **3:**10, **3:**81
Renzulli, J., **13:**18, **13:**43
Representativeness, **3:**50–51, **3:**81
Residual functioning,
    8:52–53, **8:**65
Resources
    assessment, **3:**91–93
    communication disorders,
        10:57–59
    effective instruction, **4:**75–77
    emotional disturbance, **11:**57–65
    families/community agencies,
        5:65–68
    fundamentals of special
        education, **1:**53–55
    gifted and talented child,
        13:63–65
    learning disabilities, **9:**67
    legal foundations of special
        education, **2:**65–66
    medical/physical/multiple
        disabilities, **8:**75–83
    mental retardation, **12:**81–87
    public policy/school reform,
        6:55–57
    sensory disabilities, **7:**73–85
Respondent conditioning,
    4:38, **4:**65
Response to intervention (RTI),
    9:17, **9:**18
Rheumatic fever,
    8:11 (tab), **8:**65
Rogers, C., **4:**44
Rogers, M., **4:**49
Rogers, P. A., **7:**7, **7:**11,
    7:13, **7:**14, **7:**15, **7:**34
Rose, L. C., **11:**39
Rotation errors, **3:**48
RTI (response to intervention),
    9:17, **9:**18
Rubrics, **3:**31

Rusch, F., **5:**24
Ryser, G., **7:**15

Saccuzzo, D. P., **13:**45
Safe schools, **6:**28–29
Samuelowicz, K., **4:**5
Schaller, J., **7:**15
Schattman, R., **12:**59
Schnur, E., **5:**15
School reform, **6:**19–35
    Goals 2000 (*See* Goals 2000: The
        Educate America Act)
    impact on special
        education, **6:**35
    inclusion as, **6:**21, **6:**38–39
    national goals, **6:**19–20
    national standards, **6:**30–33
    opportunity-to-learn standards,
        4:46, **6:**12, **6:**33, **6:**45
    regular education
        initiative/inclusion, **6:**21
    school restructuring,
        6:33–34, **6:**45
    See also Public policy
School restructuring,
    6:33–34, **6:**45
School-based enterprises, **5:**46, **5:**56
Schoolhouse giftedness, **13:**43, **13:**53
Schrier, E. M., **7:**36
Schumaker, J., **4:**45
Schweinhart, L., **5:**16
Screening, **3:**7–8
    defining, **3:**81
    early, **3:**8–9
    late, **3:**9–10
    tests for, **3:**28
    See also Protection in evaluation
        procedures
Section 504 of the Rehabilitation
    Act, **2:**11 (tab), **2:**13,
    2:14–15, **2:**56, **4:**54
Seizures
    grand mal (tonic-clonic),
        8:23, **8:**64
    petit mal, **8:**23, **8:**65
Self-Assessment/Answer Key
    assessment, **3:**1–3,
        3:83–85, **3:**87

communication disorders, **10**:1–5,
  10:47–51, **10**:53–54
effective instruction, **4**:1–3,
  4:67–69, **4**:71
emotional disturbance, **11**:1–3,
  11:49–51, **11**:53
families/community agencies,
  5:1–3, **5**:57–59, **5**:61
fundamentals of
  special education,
  1:1–4, **1**:45–47, **1**:49
gifted and talented child, **13**:1–3,
  13:55–57, **13**:59
learning disabilities, **9**:1–3,
  9:59–61, **9**:63
legal foundations of
  special education,
  2:1, **2**:57–60, **2**:61
medical/physical/multiple
  disabilities, **8**:1–3,
  8:67–69, **8**:71
mental retardation, **12**:1–3,
  12:73–75, **12**:77
public policy/school reform,
  6:1, **6**:47–49, **6**:51
sensory disabilities, **7**:1–3,
  7:63–65, **7**:67
Self-care, **12**:47, **12**:57
Self-contained class, **4**:28, **4**:65
Self-determination, **12**:64, **12**:72
Self-direction, **12**:46–47
Self-help skills, **3**:42
Semantics, **10**:11, **10**:44
Sensitivity errors, **3**:62
Sensorineural hearing loss, **7**:19, **7**:61
Sensory acuity, assessing,
  3:39–**3**:41 (fig)
Sensory disabilities, teaching
  student with
  assistive listening, **7**:41
  collaboration role in, **7**:52
  communication system, **7**:41–42
  cued speech, **7**:40–41
  eliminating barriers overview,
    7:34–38, **7**:35 (tab)–36 (tab),
    7:39 (tab)
  empowering student, **7**:47–48
  fostering independence, **7**:42–45
future of, **7**:52
improving communication
  overview, **7**:39 (tab)
oral communication, **7**:39–40
positive interaction tips, **7**:44–45
sign systems, **7**:40
supporting accommodations for,
  7:49–51
technology to eliminate barriers,
  7:34, **7**:36–38
telecommunication devices, **7**:41
total communication, **7**:40
understanding characteristics
  specific to, **7**:49
See also Deaf-and-blind/
  deaf-blind; Hearing
  impairments; Visual
  impairments
Sentner, S. M., **4**:5
Severe disabilities, teaching student
  with, **12**:53–59
communication considerations,
  12:56–57
community living and, **12**:57–58
curriculum considerations, **12**:56
defining severe disabilities,
  12:54–55
instructional approaches,
  12:58–59
mobility, **12**:57
prevalence of, **12**:55
self-care and, **12**:57
Shape distortions, **3**:48
Sheltered/supported employment,
  5:25, **5**:56
Shin, H., **6**:33
Siblings, effect of exceptionalities
  on, **5**:36–37
Sickle-cell anemia, **8**:11 (tab), **8**:66
Sigafoos, J., **7**:26
Sign language, **7**:39 (tab), **7**:40
Silverman, L. K., **13**:44
Singleton, P., **7**:47
Site-based management,
  6:34, **6**:35, **6**:46
Six-hour retarded child, 41
Skilled examiner, **3**:59–61
Skinner, D., **4**:5

Skull fractures, **8:**26, **8:**66
Smith, J., 14–15
Smith v. Robinson, **2:**42 (tab), **2:**47–49
Snellen Wall Chart, **3:**40
Social interactions, improving
  for student with emotional
    disturbance, **11:**13–14
  for student with learning
    disabilities, **9:**39–41
  Social problems, **11:**17, **11:**47
  Social skills, **7:**15
  occupational skills and, **3:**42
  school adaptive behavior and,
    12:45–46
  training in, **4:**47–48, **4:**65, **12:**45–46
Social values, affect on special
  education, **6:**8–10
Software
  math, **12:**41
  sight word recognition, **9:**28
Sonicguide, **4:**56
Spastic cerebral palsy, **8:**23–24
Special education
  categories of, **1:**15–17
  current reforms in, **6:**40
    (*See also* Public policy;
    School reform)
  defining, **1:**43
  future of, **6:**41
  social values and, **6:**8–10
  See also Special education,
    economic factors driving
Special education, economic factors
  driving, **6:**13–17
  allocation methods, **6:**16–17
  federal review of state
    plans, **6:**14
  funding competition, **6:**15
  OSEP programs, **6:**13–14
  research priorities, **6:**15
Special education process. *See*
  Prereferral interventions
Special educators, continuing
  demand for, **1:**20
Specific learning disabilities
  defining, **1:**17, **1:**43
  See also Learning disabilities
Spectrum disorder, **8:**29

Speece, D., **9:**17–18
Speech disorders, **10:**44
  articulation disorder, **10:**9–10
  fluency disorder, **10:**10
  voice disorder, **10:**10
Speech evaluation, **10:**44
Speech or language impairments,
  1:17, **1:**43
Speech-language pathologist,
  10:17–18, **10:**39–41, **10:**44
Spina bifida, **8:**24, **8:**66
Spinal cord injuries, **8:**24–25, **8:**66
Spooner, F., **12:**43
Stahl, S. A., **9:**28
Standard behavior chart, **4:**39, **4:**65
Standards
  defining, **6:**31, **6:**46
  legislation on, **6:**37–38
  national, **6:**30–33
  opportunity-to-learn, **4:**46, **6:**12,
    6:33, **6:**45
Stark, J., **10:**27
Stem, B., **12:**43
Stereotypes, **3:**56, **3:**81
Stern, B., **12:**43
Stern, J., **6:**13
Sternberg, R. J., **13:**43
Strabismus, **7:**10, **7:**61
Strichart, S. S., **5:**26
Structured interview, **3:**30
Stuart, M., **7:**29
Student progress records,
  4:26 (fig)–27
Stuttering. *See* Fluency disorder
Subdural hematomas, **8:**26, **8:**66
Summative evaluation, **4:**23, **4:**65
Supported employment,
  5:25, **5:**56
Swan, M., **13:**33
Syntax, **10:**10–11
Synthetic speech devices,
  7:37, **7:**62

TA (transactional analysis),
  4:44, **4:**65
Talented, defining, **13:**53
TASH (The Association for Persons
  with Severe Handicaps), **12:**55

Task analysis, **3:**22, **3:**81, **4:**10, **4:**40,
    4:65, **12:**43–45, **12:**72
Task avoidance, **11:**31–33, **11:**47
Task Force on DSM-IV, **9:**45 (tab)
Taylor, R. L., **3:**7
Teacher
    egalitarian, **4:**59–60
    highly qualified, **2:**31–32
    humanitarian, **4:**60
    radomizer, **4:**60
Teacher education/professional
    development, **6:**26–27
Teacher training, reform in, **6:**40
Teacher unit allocation
    method, **6:**16
Teaching
    defining, **4:**5, **4:**7, **4:**66
    precision, **4:**39
    principles for effective, **4:**5–6
    tips for, **6:**42
Technical career programs, **5:**45–46
Technology, to increase
    communication/motility,
    4:53–54
Technology dependent, **8:**15–16, **8:**66
Tech-prep programs,
    5:45–46, **5:**56
Telecommunication
    devices, **4:**51–52, **4:**66,
    7:39 (tab), **7:**41, **7:**42
Temper tantrums, **11:**47
Terman, L., **13:**20, **13:**41, **13:**42
Test, D. W., **12:**43
Test modifications, **4:**54
Testing/tests
    achievement, **3:**37, **3:**77
    criterion-referenced, **3:**28–29,
        3:77–78, **4:**9, **4:**64
    defining, **3:**25, **3:**81
    diagnostic, **3:**28, **3:**78
    formal, **3:**27, **3:**79
    group-administered, **3:**27, **3:**79
    group/individual tests, **3:**27
    informal measures, **3:**27
    norm-/criterion-referenced tests,
        3:28–29
    norm-referenced, **3:**29,
        3:80, **4:**9, **4:**64

screening/diagnostics, **3:**28
test content, **3:**29
test development, **3:**52–54
test fairness, **3:**55–56
test formats, **3:**27–28
test modifications, **4:**54
The Association for Persons
    with Severe Handicaps
    (TASH), **12:**55
Thematic units, **9:**57
Thinking skills, **4:**19–20
Thomas, D., **5:**15
Thurlow, M. L., **3:**71,
    5:18, **6:**9, **6:**33
Thurlow, M. L., Wiley, H. I.,
    & Bielinski, J., **6:**60
Time sampling recording,
    3:46, **3:**81
Timothy W. v. Rochester,
    New Hampshire,
    School District, **2:**5–6,
    2:42 (tab)–43 (tab)
Tinker v. Des Moines Independent
    Community School District,
    2:36 (tab)–37 (tab)
Tonic-clonic (grand mal) seizures,
    8:23, **8:**64
Total communication, for student
    with vision/hearing
    impairments, **7:**39 (tab), **7:**40
Transactional analysis
    (TA), **4:**44, **4:**65
Transition plans, **5:**17–18
    individualized, **2:**26, **2:**55–56,
        5:23, **5:**56, **12:**63, **12:**71
Transition services, **2:**26, **2:**33,
    2:56, **5:**6
    defining, **5:**23, **5:**56
    See also Community
        collaboration
Transitions
    effect on families, **5:**36–37
    See also Transition plans;
        Transition services;
        Transitions, types of
Transitions, types of, **5:**17–23
    continued education, **5:**26–27
    dropping out, **5:**20–23, **5:**21 (tab)

during school, **5:**19
employment/financial
    independence, **5:**24–25
everyday, **5:**19
post-school, **5:**23,
    5:24–25, **5:**37
preschool to K-12 education
    system, **5:**18–19
within general education
    classrooms, **5:**20
Traumatic brain injury (TBI), **1:**17,
    1:43, **8:**17, **8:**25–28, **8:**66
Tuberculosis, **8:**11 (tab), **8:**66
20/20 vision, **7:**8

Udvari-Solner, A., **12:**67
Unified system, **6:**35, **6:**46
Unstructured interview, **3:**30
U.S. Congress, **2:**16
U.S. Department of Education, **1:**11,
    1:15, **1:**19–20, **7:**10, **7:**11, **7:**21,
    7:30, **7:**56–58, **8:**6, **8:**29, **8:**34,
    9:14 (tab), **12:**11, **12:**61
U.S. Office of Civil Rights, **6:**46
Uslan, M. M., **7:**36

Validity, **3:**51–54, **3:**81
VanDeventer, P., **12:**67
Visual acuity, **3:**40, **7:**8, **7:**62
Visual functioning, **7:**10
Visual impairments, **1:**16, **1:**40
    academic/cognitive
        characteristics of,
        7:11–14, **7:**54–55
    appropriate literacy medium,
        7:16
    behavioral characteristics of,
        7:14–15
    brief history of special education
        and, **7:**7
    communication characteristics of,
        7:15–16
    defining, **7:**6, **7:**8, **7:**9, **7:**62
    eligibility for students with,
        7:9–10, **7:**55
    environmental modifications
        for, **7:**13
    focusing difficulties, **7:**9–10

physical characteristics of, **7:**14
    prevalence of, **7:**10–11, **7:**54
    signs of, **7:**12 (tab)
    teaching modifications for,
        7:13–14
    teaching tips, **7:**16 (tab)
    technological aid for, **7:**13
    visual functioning, **7:**10
Vocabulary, defining, **10:**45
Voice disorder, **10:**10, **10:**45

Wagner, M., **5:**22, **5:**24
Walker, H. M., **3:**46
Walker, R., **6:**34
Wang, M. C., **4:**31–32
Ward, M., **4:**53
Wards of court/homeless
    child, **2:**34
Warner, M., **4:**45
Washington v. Davis, **2:**39 (tab)
Watson v. City of Cambridge, Mass.,
    2:36 (tab)
Web sites (resources)
    effective instruction, **4:**75
    sensory disabilities, **7:**73
Weber, J., **11:**36
Wehman, P., **5:**44–45
Weikart, D., **5:**16
Weiss, J. A., **5:**18
Wheelchairs, **4:**56
Whole language program,
    9:27, **9:**57
Whorton, D., **4:**46
Wiederholt, L., **3:**37
Withdrawal, **3:**47, **11:**6, **11:**13
Wittrock, M. C., **4:**12
Work portfolios, **3:**31
Work-sample assessment,
    3:26, **3:**81
Written expression, improving
    checklists, **9:**33–34
    defining, **10:**45
    familiar words, **9:**34–35
    focus on quantity, **9:**33
    self-evaluation, **9:**34
    software, **9:**35
    timed exercises, **9:**35
Wyatt v. Stickney, **2:**38 (tab)

Yell, M. L., **2:**19 (fig), **2:**29, **2:**49–50

Yost, D. S., **4:**5

Young, C .L., **9:**17

Youth apprenticeships programs,
    5:45, **5:**56

Ypsilanti Perry Preschool
    Project, **5:**15–16

Ysseldyke, J. E., **3:**14,
    3:23, **3:**71, **4:**5, **5:**18,
    6:9, **6:**33, **12:**62

*Zobrest v. Catalina
    Foothills School
    District,* **2:**43 (tab)